AF266468

RELAUNCH TO WIN

A FRAMEWORK TO SUCCEED IN THE NEW NORMAL

STEPHEN FERNANDES

Relaunch To Win

Copyright © 2020 Stephen Fernandes

First published in 2020

ISBN

Paperback: 978-1-922456-14-4

E-book: 978-1-922456-15-1

All rights reserved. No part of this book may be reproduced, stored in a retrieval system, or transmitted by any means (electronic, mechanical, photocopying, recording, or otherwise) without written permission from the author.

Because of the dynamic nature of the Internet, any web addresses or links contained in this book may have changed since publication and may no longer be valid. The information in this book is based on the author's experiences and opinions. The views expressed in this book are solely those of the author and do not necessarily reflect the views of the publisher; the publisher hereby disclaims any responsibility for them.

The author of this book does not dispense any form of medical, legal, financial, or technical advice either directly or indirectly. The intent of the author is solely to provide information of a general nature to help you in your quest for personal development and growth. In the event you use any of the information in this book, the author and the publisher assume no responsibility for your actions. If any form of expert assistance is required, the services of a competent professional should be sought.

Publishing information

Publishing, design, and production facilitated by Passionpreneur Publishing, A division of Passionpreneur Organization Pty Ltd, ABN: 48640637529

www.PassionpreneurPublishing.com

Melbourne, VIC | Australia

To my dearest parents, Benadicta and Robert,
"You taught me how to dream by dreaming for me. You taught
me how to believe by believing in me. Your sacrifices and love
will always remain the foundation of who I am."

Testimonials

Stephen has that rare, brilliant philosopher mind to reflect, observe, and learn from people around us and their lives. His simple, yet profound observations modelled into a framework will serve as a personal transformation guide to many and help the world heal from the most difficult period in history after the wars...

—Subramanian Venkatramani, Chief Mentor and Founder, Cerebrum Digital, India

Stephen's insights and experiences shine through in this book with great tools to "Relaunch and Win." There is a clarity of thought and purpose that comes through in his writing with a blueprint to achieve success and scale higher.

—Faisal Usman, Director Global Delivery Model Services, PWC, Florida, USA

I have known Stephen from childhood and have witnessed his professional education and his successful journey in the corporate world. I have witnessed continuous improvement and transformation in his life, be on the soccer field or the various positions he held during his career. Stephen is a true success story, applying the very principles that he uses and now shares them with the world.

—Dr. Sean George (MBBS, MD, MACP, FRACP), Australia

I have known Stephen for over 30 years and have witnessed his natural ability to adapt and transform. I am thrilled he has leveraged his experience and derived ReLaunch X, which will undoubtedly help transform people's lives.

—Yatin Rao, Industry Professional with *Fortune* 100 Company, Silicon Valley, California, USA

Delighted that this is a book dedicated to those wanting to change and looking for ways to do it. A hands-on book that helps people overcome the anxiety of change in their personal and professional sphere and take decisions needed to succeed in the New-Normal! Kudos to Stephen to bring this out while it is most needed.

—Prof. Dayanand M S, Professor & Vice Dean (Research), Goa Business School, Goa University, Goa, India

I have known Stephen for over 30 years and have always admired his ability to take stock of his current environment and adapt to the changes and challenges that lay ahead. With ReLauch X, Stephen leverages his experience to provide valuable insight and tools to reboot and advance your career.

—Aldrich Almeida, Industry Professional, *Fortune* 100 Company, Portland Oregon, USA

Continuous disruption to our lives — personal and professional — is the new normal. Stephen has simplified and presented a framework to succeed in this book.

—Kunal Goklany, Director Operations & Technology, Citi, London, United Kingdom

I have worked with Stephen and have been impressed with his natural ability to adapt and transform to meet his goals. I am happy that he has now shared his learnings through this book to help others.

**—Tassos Kazinos, Chief Executive Officer,
Trastor REIC, Greece**

Stephen is a prolific writer and wonderful coach. Relaunch X is a transformative tool for readers to achieve and sustain success by way of understanding thyself to adapt to the new normal. I am extremely happy that he has translated his experiences into words for the benefit of the greater good. I am sure Relaunch will not be a book to read but a guiding memoir in many lives in the future.

**—Dr. Senthil Nathan Thirugnana Sambandam,
CEO, Phanes Biotech, USA**

Relaunch To Win makes a powerful case for the rapid transformation required in our lives today. The journey of purpose with continuous improvement and growth is very well imbibed in the "ReLaunch X" framework.

**—Dr. Dhrupad Mathur, Deputy Director—Faculty
Management; Associate Professor—ITM,
SP Jain School of Global Management
(India)**

Stephen's rich experience in the IT sector along with his ability to analyse the peaks and troughs of life, through ReLaunch X, will be insightful to anyone wishing to adopt the winning ways of life.

—Jeetendra Nayak, Entrepreneur and Managing Director for Ankseals Pvt. Ltd., Minar Hydrosystems Pvt. Ltd., and Minerva Automotors Pvt. Ltd., Nagpur, Maharashtra, India

This book shows the importance of self-directed and lifelong learning. To be successful, in this rapidly changing world, it is important to be innovative and a change master.

—Dr. Ismail A.S. Burud, Senior Lecturer in Surgery, Head Division of Surgery, International Medical University, Kuala Lumpur, Malaysia

Motivating, inspirational. Failure never felt so rewarding, nor success so sweet. A must-read for those who want to be successful. The book serves as an ideal launching pad to fulfil your dreams.

—Dr. Prakash Pania, Consultant Endocrinologist, Aster Jubilee Medical Complex, Dubai, UAE

Stephen is an inspirational leader, with a highly personal style. He builds enduring relationships, offering valuable advice to clients, as well as those of us who have had the pleasure to work with him. I look forward to applying his "ReLaunch X" success secrets.

—Peter Steward, Head of UK Organisational Change Management Consulting, Cognizant, United Kingdom

Stephen is a good friend and guide to have by your side if one wishes to make their career journey successful. His enthusiasm for challenges and perseverance are key attributes that would make a difference to anyone keen on transforming themselves and learn through a dependable guide.

—Prabu Balasubramanian, Co-Founder & Executive Director, TransSys Solutions, Dubai, UAE

The book is an excellent directional guide to transform and relaunch life. Steering in the right direction and staying relevant in the new normal world is impressively articulated by Stephen and makes the book an incredibly good read.

—Namrta Srivastava, General Manager, Legal, Leading Telecom Company, India

Contents

Acknowledgement xiii
About the Author xv

Introduction 1
Chapter One   The Roller-Coaster Ride 7
Chapter Two   Great Success Is Built On Failures 15
Chapter Three   Phase 1—Assess 25
  3.1 Start with Where 27
  3.2 Assess You 31
  3.3 Manage Your FUD Factor—Manage Fear
      to Manage Your Uncertainty and Doubt 41
  3.4 Find Your Life Purpose 51
  3.5 Tools to Assess 59
Chapter Four   Phase 2—Align 65
  4.1 Establish Your Goals 67
  4.2 Understand Your Points of Inflection 85
  4.3 Power of Your Visualisation 91
  4.4 Build Your Mastermind by Gaining Mindshare 99
  4.5 Align Your Body, Mind, and Soul (BMS) 105
  4.6 Realign with Your Constraints 107
  4.7 Your Personal Development Plan (PDP) 113
  4.8 Tools to Align 115
Chapter Five   Phase 3—Transform 119
  5.1 Align Transformation to Your Life Purpose 121
  5.2 Understand the Change Process . . . To Embrace It 127
  5.3 Overhaul Your Habits . . . Replace Old with
      New Habits 137

5.4   Leverage Your Strengths . . . To Progress   143
5.5   Commit to Continuous Learning . . .
        Differentiate with Knowledge and Skills   147
5.6   Manage Your Energy Levels . . .
        For High Productivity and Results   151
5.7   Manage Your Time . . . Have a Daily Ritual   157
5.8   Manage Your Health . . . For High Performance   163
5.9   Build Your Safety Net . . . By Securing Financially   167
5.10 Build Your Personal Network . . . Be a Propellant   179
5.11 You Are a Product of Yourself   189
5.12 Establish the Personal Brand Called "You"   195

Chapter Six   Phase 4—Measure and Monitor   **201**
6.1   Need to Measure   203
6.2   How to Measure   207
6.3   Monitor Your Environment   217
6.4   Manage Risks to Mitigate   221
6.5   Know Your Delta   225

Chapter Seven   Phase 5—Relaunch   **231**
7.1   Manage Your Delta to Retain Control   233
7.2   The "X" in "ReLaunch X"   237
7.3   The Art of Follow Up   241
7.4   Self-Manage to Relaunch   245

Conclusion   **253**
Bibliography   **259**

Acknowledgement

My journey to write this book started in 2015. What started out as notes for my two lovely children, Nadia and Nathan, culminated into a book. The sparks within me were ignited and reinforced as my business technology articles got published in the Tech Talk section of the *Gulf News*. There were several occasions when I thought that I would never get through this book, but my perseverance and focus were reinforced by the deep desire of sharing my learnings with the people who need it the most.

I thank my wife, Manisha, for supporting me in reviewing the book draft. Her valuable inputs, along with the feedback from my children, helped me add the final touches to my book.

I thank my brother, Agnelo, who continues to energise me with his inspiring thoughts and perspectives.

I thank my ex-colleague and good friend, Ketan Bhagat, who had been instrumental in sharing his learnings on what it takes to write and, more importantly, to complete a book.

I thank my childhood friend from school and college, Faisal Usman, who reviewed my book draft and shared his valuable feedback.

I thank all my school, engineering and management alumni who continue to inspire and support each other, including me, much like an extended global family. There is still so much to learn from each other.

My special thanks to the leadership and publishing team at Passionprenuer for their enthusiasm, patience, and guidance in helping me complete the last mile of this journey.

About the Author

Stephen Fernandes is an accomplished professional working in Information Technology (IT) for nearly three decades. His experience includes working for Fortune Global 500, Forbes Global 2000 companies, family-owned conglomerates, and start-ups across markets.

As an early evangelist and proponent of digital transformation in the Middle East, he actively engages with clients and other stakeholders in pursuing their transformation journey. As a thought leader, he presented at several IT forums including Gartner Symposium and IDC CIO Summit. He authored several business technology articles in the Tech Talk section of the *Gulf News*, UAE.

Stephen successfully established and led global, local, and start-up IT companies in the Middle East, in addition to being a part of several mergers and acquisitions and joint venture initiatives. He grew and managed multimillion-dollar businesses by creating successful "Go To Market" strategies and building high-performing teams and trusted client relationships. With a consultative-led approach, he headed and won several IT transformations. His business experience spans across several industries, which include retail, consumer, banking, telecom, travel, transportation, healthcare, and hospitality. He launched and led several innovative marketing and branding initiatives to significantly improve brand equity.

Stephen is a skilled thought leader with deep knowledge of markets and culture. He is a strategist and a critical thinker with outstanding communication, presentation, and mentoring skills. In his professional career, he interacted with and witnessed several leaders transforming not only themselves but also their companies and the people around them. He learned firsthand by engaging with entrepreneurs, chairpersons, board members, chief executive officers, presidents, chief financial officers, chief information officers, directors, peers, colleagues, young graduates, alumni, family, friends, and aspiring individuals. He closely observed what it takes to bounce back to success from each failure.

By engaging with various leaders over the years, he gained deep insights into their thought processes and derived a simple success approach for others to achieve their success. He learned and observed that some people are more successful than others, but the fundamental remains the same—they all have a common pattern to their success. They proactively transform, by continuously improving themselves, to stay relevant in their ecosystem, thereby ensuring they not only grow but also thrive in this new age economy. He is a firm believer that all people are resourceful and their path to success lies untapped within themselves. They need to believe in themselves, discover their passion, and relentlessly execute on following their life's purpose.

Stephen holds a master's in management studies and a bachelor's in engineering. He is a Certified Global Business Leader (CGBL) from Harvard Business School Publishing and a "Professionally Trained Coactive Coach" from the Coaches Training Institute (CTI). He relocated to the Middle East in 1997 and has been living with his family in Dubai for nearly two decades. He has travelled extensively to over thirty countries across the globe and had the opportunity to work with people from different markets, industries, professions, and cultures.

visit www.stephenfernandes.com

Introduction

Be thankful for what you have; you'll end up having more. If you concentrate on what you don't have, you will never have enough.

—Oprah Winfrey

You are a winner! Yes, a Winner!

We all are winners and have won many times in our lives. As you read this book, you are either already successful and want to keep winning or facing a temporary setback and want to win again. Either way, you will come out a winner in the new normal. Start with "believing you can... and you will".

Everyone is born with a purpose. They need to discover their life purpose that lies dormant within them and then relentlessly work towards fulfiling it. Successes and failures are an integral part of our life. One precedes the other like the day precedes the night. On the one hand, successes drive us to greater heights and must be consistently sustained with the required efforts. On the other hand, failures provide the learnings and life experiences needed to become successful. They are the stepping-stones to achieve success. Accepting failures as a part of your life, making peace with yourself, and learning from them, sets the stage for being successful.

The need to change is a constant challenge faced by individuals. The new normal is not only driving them to change but also to transform rapidly. This change and transformation is either driven internally by the individual, in a proactive, planned manner, or is forced upon them by unprecedented external events, in a disruptive manner. Rapidly embracing change and swiftly adapting to transformation is what makes them winners.

Successful people do things differently and do them consistently. They have a secret formula to succeed not just once but repeatedly and consistently. They are driven by a clear sense of purpose and relentlessly pursue their dreams and aspirations. They are masters of their own destiny—proactive and energised, internally fulfilled, and in control of their outcomes, like a self-mastery leader.

Why the book on ReLaunch To Win

The last decade was led by digitalisation, thereby establishing a digitalised economy. The digital disruption affected people's livelihood, their jobs, roles, and positions—the way they worked, communicated, and engaged with their employees, customers, suppliers, and partners. This also disrupted the way they engaged with their family and socialised with their friends. Digitalisation forced people to change, enhance their knowledge, skills, and competency, or else risk being made irrelevant. Yesterday's skilled employees were not guaranteed their jobs in today's new skilled digital economy, driven by continuous innovation to the business and operating models. While it made companies extinct and people redundant, it also created new industries, companies, jobs, and positions. The rate of digital adoption varied from industry to industry and from country to country.

The year 2020 witnessed another disruption led by the pandemic (COVID-19). The scale of this disruption is seemingly unmeasurable, due to the constant change across ecosystems. On the one hand, the pandemic disruption forced the shutdown of economies, industries, and companies, sadly leading to millions of job losses and forced unemployment. Ironically, on the other hand, it fueled the adoption of digitalisation across all aspects of our life with Work from Home, Play at Home, Learn from Home, Teach from Home, and Perform from Home, among others, driven largely by the need to stay connected.

The **digital disruption** and the **pandemic disruption** have now converged to form our **"new normal."** This has forever changed the way we engage and the future of work. In this new normal, change is the only constant, where people have no control over the micro/macro-economic factors affecting them. That said, they can undoubtedly control how they relaunch themselves into the new normal by swiftly assessing their current position and aligning and transforming themselves to achieve their new goals.

Interestingly, today's population represents different strata of generations. They include baby boomers born between 1946 and 1964, Generation X born between 1965 and 1979, Generation Y born between 1980 and 1994, and Generation Z born between 1995 and 2010. Their priorities, needs, outlook to work and life, and demands from family, friends, and society differ vastly from each other. Each generation has its unique traits and follows a unique pattern. Baby boomers and Gen X tend to be more frugal and financially stable. Gen Y and Gen Z have lived through disruptive changes both technologically and economically, and they are more receptive to change as a way of life.

People in the new age economy face a unique situation. That is, how do they transform and grow to bring about sustained success in their lives. The rapid pace of change in this new age economy adds further complexity to their situation, pushing them to not only change but to also transform rapidly and adapt to the new normal. This rapid transformation is required for their survival and growth.

The challenges faced by individuals living in the new normal can be addressed by adopting a five-phased framework called **"ReLaunch X."** This demands an understanding of oneself and establishing an alignment with the new age economy by applying the five phases of "ReLaunch X"—Assess, Align, Transform, Monitor & Measure, and Relaunch, as a way of life. ReLaunch X calls for people to take the first step towards a progressive and positive change. This starts by resetting their minds, knowing their life purpose, and recalibrating their journey to achieve their life purpose.

This book started as a reference guide for my two children to share my learnings and experiences gained over the last three decades. It has primarily focussed on individual transformation, adding perspectives where possible to organisational transformation by tapping into my experience to unearth the patterns that made people successful. This book is a companion to help people shift from their current state to a successful or a more successful state. It is based on the principle of continuous improvement of your current state and being proactively prepared to progress in your life journey. If a person is successful, then how do they stay successful and achieve more? If a person has failed, then how do they shift from failure to success?

The learnings from this book can be applied to any aspect of your life. It can be adopted and applied by anyone, including entrepreneurs, directors, managers, employers, employees, unemployed, graduates, students, parents, and others. This book will aid anyone who seeks to grow by continuously improving themselves and raising their standards. This book is for people who want to succeed in life and live their dreams in fulfilment of their life purpose.

There are millions of people out there who are struggling in the new normal. They could do with help to guide them through their difficult times and lead them to success. I feel the ache in my heart for people across the world who are undergoing highly disruptive and turbulent times in their lives as an outcome of the COVID-19 pandemic. This inspired me to complete the book, so I could play my role, even if in a small way, to help people out there to bounce back to their new normal.

Congratulations on picking up this book! You have taken the first step towards transforming yourself into the new normal. This is a thought-provoking book, so grab a pencil and keep capturing your ideas and thoughts, completing the exercises before moving on to the next chapter. To maximise your investment in time, I urge you to read this book with a beginner's mindset, allowing your mind to be inspired with new thoughts. Commit to adopting the learnings from this book and applying the principles to your daily life.

This book will transform you if you allow for it. As you discover yourself and transform, share your learnings with your family, friends, and colleagues. This will not only give them the joy of accepting the transformed you but will also give you the joy of touching their lives and in the process, help transforming them.

Chapter One

The Roller-Coaster Ride

> *Life's too short to dwell on things. When you go through experiences that are bad, it's a good thing. You learn from it—become a stronger person. Life is a roller coaster, and you don't know what's going to be thrown at you next, so all you can do is give it your best shot.*
>
> *—Alesha Dixon*

Don, in his mid-thirties, aspired to be an author, but met with an unfortunate accident that left him blind. His life was seemingly shattered. He mustered all his strengths, without letting himself down, and in a few months, he learned how to walk with the help of his cane. In a few years, he trained himself to be a braillewriter and reader for the visually impaired. He did not stop there; several years later, he transformed his life to be more purposeful and fulfiling by authoring books for the blind. His persistence and positive approach towards his tragedy not only helped him fulfil his life purpose but also helped touch other people's life.

Sariah is an entrepreneur who failed, not once but several times, only to bounce back each time and take the necessary steps forward to fulfil her goals. Despite repeatedly failing, she was determined to lift herself and continue her journey. She used every failure that came her way as a new learning experience and did not let these failures prevent her from progressing. She is now a multimillionaire, supporting young, aspiring women entrepreneurs not only as an angel investor but also as an advisor, sharing her valuable experiences with them.

What drove these people to pursue their success paths? It is having a life purpose that subconsciously pushed them to complete their journey. Their resonance with their life purpose lifted them each time they failed, and it reinforced their approach each time they succeeded. They tapped into their inner energy and converted it into outer energy (actions) to progress forward in pursuit of their life purpose.

The roller-coaster ride

Have you been on a roller-coaster ride or seen someone take a roller-coaster ride? The experience is a heart-pounding one, at least for the first few rides. The experience of the high speed, the unexpected highs and lows, the thrills, and fears with every sharp turn gives you an adrenaline rush with a fast-pounding heartbeat. The first ride is always a memorable experience and remains etched in your brain, like a childhood memory.

No matter how many subsequent rides you take on that roller coaster, the thrills, excitement, and anxiety would never match your first ride. The first ride is truly distinct and unique in many ways. You tend to compare the subsequent rides with the first ride.

The thrills and anxiety of going down the roller coaster are so different from climbing up the roller coaster. As you go up the roller coaster ride, there is a sense of anticipation and preparedness. You instinctively begin to anticipate and mentally prepare for the fall and the sharp turn that is to follow. You tighten your body while firmly gripping the handlebar of the roller coaster. The feeling of going down the roller coaster is like a freewheeling dive with the gravitational force behind it.

As you repeatedly embark on the same roller-coaster ride, you begin to develop a sense of comfort and ease with every additional ride. The initial anxiety of taking the ride disappears. This comes from knowing what highs and lows to anticipate, what speed and sharp turns to expect, and to predict when the journey ends. You begin to enjoy the subsequent rides in a more comforting way. The comfort comes from having been through the same ride earlier. Your brain shifts its thinking and functioning from an unexpected-conscious state to an expected-conscious state, as this becomes a familiar journey and you now know what to expect.

From my childhood memories, I recall a friend who had severe anxiety before embarking on his first roller-coaster ride. His fears amplified further by noticing the children around us who were equally anxious. While standing in the queue, we figured the best way to overcome this anxiety was to watch the roller-coaster ride from the outside, so that we know what we were getting into by the time we boarded the ride. By doing so, my friend could visualise his ride ahead of time. When it was our turn to board the roller-coaster ride, we had already formed a motion picture of the ride in our minds. This eased his anxiety, and we both enjoyed the ride.

Life is like a roller-coaster ride, having unexpected changes in acceleration and directions. The roller-coaster ride can be thrilling or frightening. It all depends on your perspective of the ride. If your perspective is to mentally enjoy the thrills and excitement of the ride, you will enjoy the ride, no matter what. If you are not mentally prepared to enjoy the ride, due to the inherent fear and uncertainty, you are unlikely to enjoy the ride. Your perception of the ride will make all the difference. In life, your proactive preparedness to deal with the difficult times will ensure that you come out as a winner.

Your roller-coaster ride could be anything like your new job, moving to a new role, relocating to a new country, starting a new business, buying a house, preparing for an undergraduate or postgraduate course, or becoming a parent, among others. Whatever it may be, you must proactively prepare for your life journey ahead. Higher your preparation, the lower will be your stress and the higher will be your probability of a successful journey with fulfilment and happiness.

The life journey most individuals and organisations experience is like this roller-coaster ride. You could keep watching other people ride and wonder what their experience must have been, or you could proactively prepare, embrace the ride yourself, and enjoy the experience. This ride differs from individual to individual and company to company. Some people take this ride feeling petrified, while others take this ride prepared—gaining confidence and embarking on their subsequent rides.

Life is a journey of highs and lows. With every low, there is a high, and with every high, there could be a low. The question is, how do you move from a low to a high and how do you maintain your high, while proactively preparing to ride the lows as and when they come. Embracing life's unexpected twists and turns prepares us to deal with them. The better prepared you are, both mentally and physically with knowledge and skills, the more equipped you will be to take on life.

Some individuals are fortunate to experience a high phase of life where everything is near perfect. Their work life is well balanced;

they spend quality time with their families, while their financial position is secured. On the other hand, some individuals have been less fortunate to experience a drought period in their lives and their financial situation could get worse, with the load of debts and loans to be paid. The fortunate individuals identified their goals, assessed where they were, and then transformed themselves to reach their goals. They were alert to the new developments that came along their way and proactively prepared themselves for life's roller-coaster ride ahead. They were smart to grab the new opportunities that life offered, while avoiding the pitfalls. The less fortunate individuals are probably those who did not prepare for what was to come and hence were left in despair.

Organisations are no different from individuals. Some companies are fortunate to experience consistent growth in revenues, profitability, and market share, backed by strong customer and employee satisfaction. On the other hand, some companies have been less fortunate to experience an unprecedented decline in revenues and profitability with a looming threat of bankruptcy. What differentiates successful organisations is their ability to proactively sense and assess their present situation, visualise an image of their future state (vision and mission), and transform themselves into that future state image. They proactively detect early warning signs of change to their ecosystems and respond in a timely manner. These could be changes brought on by new customer demands, geopolitical changes, environmental changes, the rising challenge of unknown competitors, or even pandemics. The unknown competitors are those who land overnight in the incumbent's market only to destroy the status quo and win market share in a short span of time.

The new normal defined by the new age economy has no fixed rules; the survival of the fittest depends on their speed, agility, and ability to transform while frequently adapting on an ongoing basis. Generations have witnessed several phases of economic shifts right from the labor-intensive economy, to the industrialised economy, to the knowledge economy, and to the digitalised economy. The consistent ingredients for survival across these economic metamorphoses have been the ability to anticipate, prepare, innovate, and differentiate with rapid adaptability to change. Both individuals and organisations that have been quick to respond have thrived with unprecedented growth.

Exercise:
Answer the below questions to help you build your own roller-coaster perspective.

1. Think of your last roller-coaster ride (new job, relocating, new businesses, etc.).
2. What were your challenges?
3. What did you learn from the ride?
4. How did you adapt to the new situation?
5. In retrospect, would you do things differently?
6. What is your present roller-coaster ride?
7. What is your level of preparedness?
8. What is your plan to complete this roller-coaster ride?

Chapter Two

Great Success Is Built On Failures

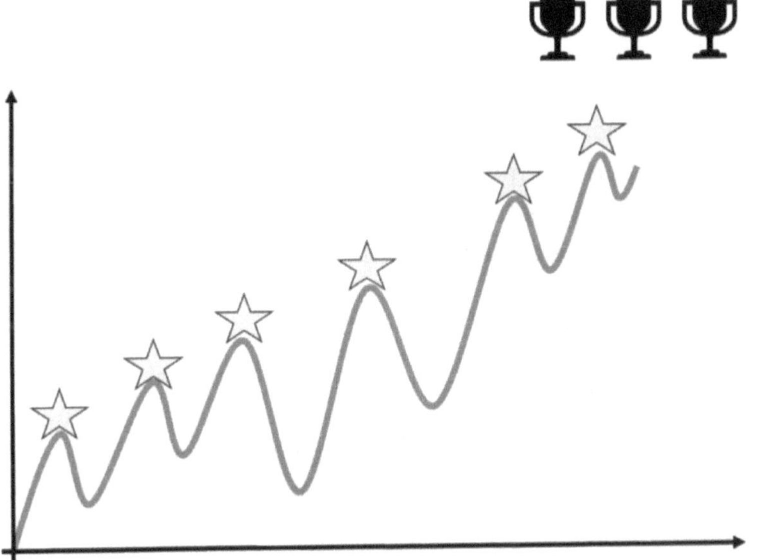

> *Failure is so important. We speak about success*
> *all the time. But it is the ability to resist or use*
> *failure that often leads to greater success.*

> —*J. K. Rowling*

Both success and failure pose their own unique set of challenges. On the one hand, the challenge for people who have succeeded is how they can continue to grow and succeed consistently. On the other hand, the challenge for people who have failed is how to overcome their failures and shift to being successful.

Newton's first law of motion states that *if a body is at rest or moving at a constant speed in a straight line, it will remain in this state unless acted upon by an external force.* The key point to note here is that an external force is required to change the state of motion. Both success and failure need a force to either remain in a successful state or to overcome the failed state.

If a person is in a failed state, he or she would continue to remain in a failed state unless acted upon by an external force. In this context, the external force is a combination of your mind and soul acting upon your body to move it to a success state. Success, if not proactively managed, could slip to failures, and failures, if not acted upon, would continue to remain in the status quo.

Most people experience both successes and failures in their life. Successes make people feel good about themselves and increase their self-worth and self-esteem while driving them to achieve more and progress to greater heights. Success means different things to different people, likewise with failures. They are both linked to a person's definition of happiness. It is imperative to understand and appreciate that both these states form a part of life, and how they are perceived will play a pivotal role in shaping one's life.

Failure could be perceived as a learning experience where one gains real-life valuable experience, or it could be perceived as a deep, dark tunnel with no light at the end of it. Perceptions are derived from self-belief, mindset, values, knowledge, and past experiences. Mindset is key; one should choose to have a progressive mindset and derive a positive learning experience from the situation and thereby gain valuable insights for their journey ahead.

Walt Disney was fired from Kansas City Star, apparently as he lacked imagination and creativity. He attempted to launch several of his own businesses, none of which were successful and left him bankrupt. His wisdom to learn from his past failures, self-belief to follow his life purpose, and dedication to follow his dreams made him a legend for generations to come. His persistence led him to create the world's largest entertainment theme park, which not only entertains children and families but also generates billions of dollars.

Experiencing or witnessing failures is a blessing, mostly in disguise, as these are great teachers. They teach people to value the things taken for granted, understand what led to their failures, how to proactively avoid the same failures in the future, and more importantly, what needs to be done to rise from a failed state. The lessons learned from failures get etched in their memory bank. *Steven Spielberg* was rejected multiple times by the University of Southern California, School of Cinematic Art. He went on to complete over twenty-five movies; received three Academy

Awards, four Emmys, and seven Daytime Emmys, and amassed wealth of billions of dollars.

There cannot be a greater combination than to have a great teacher with a brilliant student. This is what failure offers you; it is a great teacher. All you must do is be that diligent student and learn from the past failures, reinforce these learnings, and proactively apply them in your journey ahead. As Bill Gates said, "Success is a lousy teacher. It seduces smart people into thinking they can't lose."

Do not let failures hold you back from pursuing your journey. Detach the emotions associated with past failures to allow yourself to learn from them and progress. You cannot control attributes that are outside your circle of influence. That said, you can and must control the attributes that are within your circle of influence. Place your life purpose and goals in front of you; focus your efforts on marshalling your resources to win while preparing for any unprecedented eventualities that may come your way.

What is ReLaunch X?

ReLaunch X will help individuals to bounce back from their unsuccessful state or situation and more importantly enable them to remain consistently successful. They need to take the necessary steps towards relaunching themselves not once, but consistently on an ongoing basis. It should be a way of life.

ReLaunch X is like a smart algorithm. The more regularly you use it and make it a part of your daily life, the better equipped you will be to move forward in your life. In today's world, algorithm-based apps, such as Facebook, Instagram, Twitter, LinkedIn, Snapchat, Uber, Airbnb, and others, rely on their customer's data fed into them to become smarter and intelligent. Likewise with your higher adoption of ReLaunch X, it captures more data about you, giving you better insights into your life purpose, the improvements you need to make, the resources that can help you, and how you will reach your stated goals.

ReLaunch X gets smarter and becomes consistently effective with more iterative loops it completes. The process of repeatedly relaunching oneself led to the name "ReLaunch X," where X is the number of *Relaunch Improvement Loops* (RIL) or *continuous improvement loops* required to be acted upon to achieve continued success. With continuous adoption, ReLaunch X becomes hyperpersonalised to you, leveraging your strengths to meet your goals and life purpose. The concept of the ReLaunch X loop is explained in the latter part of this book.

The ReLaunch X framework has five phases. These include *Assess, Align, Transform, Monitor & Measure, and Relaunch* that help to achieve your goals and fulfil your life purpose. Each of the five phases of ReLaunch X is detailed in the subsequent chapters.

The ReLaunch X Framework

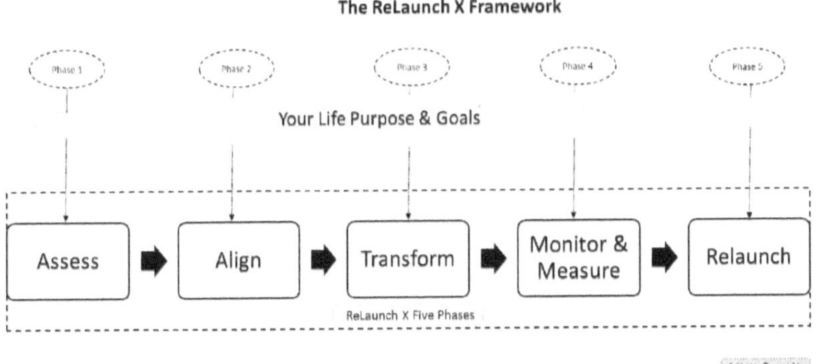

Subject to Copyright

To be successful consistently, one needs to proactively focus on continuously improving the current state. Find out what can be done better, learn how it can be done better, and identify who can help to get it done faster. Adapting to change with an open mind will set you on a path of rapid progress.

Origin of ReLaunch X

Having heard the word "Relaunch" several times, you must be wondering about the origin of the name. First, no matter what state an individual or organisation is in, they can pick themselves up and launch themselves. Second, we live in a world where nothing is constant except change. You need to launch yourself not once or twice but on an ongoing basis, depending on which aspect of your life you want to change. Your ability to not just launch but to repeatedly relaunch yourself on your journey is what will differentiate you. Third and the most important is your undeterred commitment and decision to take the first step to relaunch yourself.

To relaunch, you need to initiate with your life purpose firmly placed in the centre and an unconditional commitment to continuous self-improvisation, no matter what challenges or difficulties you face. Your mind will subconsciously act and relaunch your actions in an auto mode. Mastering ReLaunch X prepares you for the journey ahead. ReLaunch X is intended to help you find the magic in you to make it happen.

Some questions may surface in your mind: When is the best time to start? Does it depend on my profession and age? Can it be used across all aspects of my life? The answer to all these questions and several more is that ReLaunch X is a universal model, built on the natural forces of continuous self-improvement that lie dormant within you. You need a conscious state of mind to know your present situation, a structured approach, the discipline to execute and continuously improve, and the persistence to stay the course.

Anytime is the best time to begin and adopt ReLaunch X, the key being that the principles should be applied continuously and consistently. Each phase of ReLaunch X is a precursor to the next phase. They need to be followed with undeterred rigour, commitment, and discipline to launch yourself to the next orbit.

ReLaunch X was developed under the theme "simplifying complexities." As human beings, we either tend to overcomplicate our situations or we tend to get overwhelmed by the scale of the situation. We end up cluttering our thought process and complicating our approach. A simple approach followed with rigour and discipline is required to achieve your goals.

ReLaunch X for individuals

On the one hand, some individuals reach a stage where they are at low self-esteem; they feel grounded and their brains freeze. Their brains stop functioning and their energies are diverted in a maze of negative thoughts. They begin to doubt themselves and their capabilities. Their confidence slides down, lowering their self-esteem. The once-all-confident person is lost and forgotten in them; the images of past successes get erased from their memories. They begin to have a failed image of themselves, further lowering their confidence. They come to a virtual standstill with decelerated or no progress. ReLaunch X can be applied by them to bring about the necessary shift and help them back on track towards success.

On the other hand, some other individuals are fortunate to have high self-esteem. However, they reach a stage where they get into an incompetent saturation mode. Over time, being in this monotonous state, they drift away from the realities of what got them there. They slip into complacency or oblivion and a state of saturated competency. By the time realisation sets in, they could be in a descending mode on a downward trajectory. ReLaunch X can be timely applied to halt their descent and bring them back to an upward trajectory in their lives.

ReLaunch X for organisations

This phenomenon is not too different for organisations. The life of an organisation is determined by the life of its leadership team, products, customers, employees and partners. We have witnessed incumbent industry leaders helplessly surrendering their position to start-ups as a result of their shortsightedness towards newborn competitors, who disrupted their status quo overnight. They believed their competitors were remodelling themselves out of weakness towards adopting a defensive strategy. These companies were driving with their blinders on, oblivious to the prevailing market realities, customer preferences, competitive landscape, and changes both within their organisation and outside the ecosystem. The principles of the ReLaunch X can be applied by these organisations to support their win-back strategy and regain lost ground.

Increasingly, start-ups have an inherent DNA and confidence in knowing what it takes to launch a concept from idea to execution phase. They are quick to onboard investors onto their ideas and launch their business within a short period. Along the way, they come across several points of inflection and naively ignore them, at their own peril, leading to their downward trajectory. The smarter start-ups have leveraged these inflection points and changed course to meet the vision of their founders and stakeholders. The principles of ReLaunch X can be adopted by them to drive continuous improvement, which in turn will drive improvements in their products and strategy.

No matter what role an individual presently plays in life, managing themselves is the fundamental step needed in pursuit of their goals. Successful individuals and organisations first lead themselves, and then lead others.

Exercise:

1. Build and maintain a log of all your success stories across all aspects of your life.
2. Maintain a learning log (from your failures) to make sure you capture and apply your learning to your next success.
3. Ask yourself the question, "Knowing what I now know, how would I do it differently?"

Chapter Three

Phase 1 — Assess

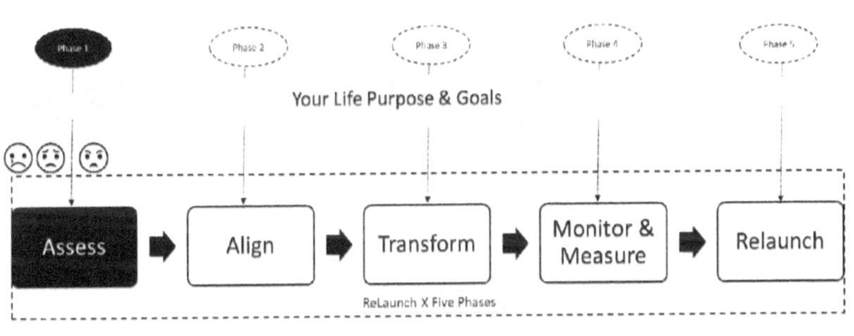

3.1 Start with Where

*There is a luxury in self-reproach. When we
blame ourselves, we feel that no one else has a
right to blame us.*

—Oscar Wilde

The past is just that, the past; learn from it and move on. People tend to get emotionally attached to their past. Past failures tend to bog them down with needless analysis paralysis undermining their capability, self-esteem, and confidence. They try to understand "why" things went wrong and why they did not see it coming, why did they not prepare, why . . . This freezes their mind into an analysis mode with the risk of allowing negative thoughts to enter their minds, thereby impacting their self-esteem.

People forget their inborn instincts. For centuries, this is what helped humans survive the brutal environment. Our instincts intuitively tell us when danger is approaching or when our businesses, positions, or jobs are at risk. We instinctively know when the dynamics around us are about to change. It may be another aspect that one may or may not choose to acknowledge and act upon it. We instinctively know when our position in the market is being threatened or a potential opportunity may arise. We may choose to ignore these threats, developing an ostrich-like mentality hoping that the threat passes away without causing any damage, or we may be smart to capitalise on the opportunity. The key to sustaining our instincts is knowing where we are and remaining alert to the development both within and outside our ecosystem.

Successful leaders have a clear vision. They know where they are at any given point in time, where they want to go, and how they will get there. Recollect the great migrations when tribes migrated from one location to another. Tribal leaders knew where they were, where they wanted to go, what resources they would need, and how they would go about their journey. They would find a place close to the seacoast where their tribes or communities could settle down, start their business, and conduct trade with ease at a lower cost and faster time to transport. They had a vision of what they wanted to build and how they would go about it with a clear goal in mind.

What matters is what lies ahead of you, not behind you. You must ascertain "where" you are today (your current state) before you move forward (your future state). It is important to assess and understand your present situation and to know how happy you are. Determine your current location coordinates and where you presently are in your life. Starting with the question "where" will enable you to assess and measure where you are at the moment, how far you have reached or are yet to reach in your journey, how much have you achieved or are yet to achieve, and whether you are on track or offtrack towards achieving your goals. Are you on your own journey or a journey that belongs to someone else?

Your location coordinates
Once you have locked down your present location coordinates, focus on "where you want to be"—that is, your future state across

a specific aspect of your life. If you have chosen wealth, write down where you would like to be with regards to your personal finances. The future state is your North star. Your North star will guide you throughout your journey. The North star is your life purpose; you just need to follow it. Our minds are tuned to follow a guidance system. Either we preprogram it with the end destination, or it follows any other guidance system closest to influencing it.

You can call it your inner global positioning system (GPS), similar to the GPS you would use in your car and follow the directions it provides to reach your end destination. Once you program your mind with the end destination, it subconsciously navigates the path towards it. Your inner GPS or inner navigation system gets smarter over time and seamlessly guides you in the right direction. You need to have the discipline to follow its directions.

Ironically, most people are yet to identify their purpose; they take each day as it comes, and hope to have better days. They are busy being busy and never seem to have the time for themselves. They do not have a clear sense of what they want to achieve and what resonates with them. In the absence of a life purpose, they are living and working for someone else's life purpose. The "someone else" are the successful people. It is imperative for you to have a life purpose and reestablish your goals. You must update your goals regularly to ensure they remain relevant to your life purpose.

Take a few minutes to capture your thoughts and answer these questions to help you understand where you are and where you want to go:

1. Where am I today?
2. Where do I want to be or go?
3. Where in my life journey have I reached today?
4. How far am I from achieving my goals?
5. Where would I find the resources to help me?

Having asked yourself the *where* question, the next step is to answer *what you want to achieve* and *how you will achieve it*.

3.2 Assess You

To find yourself, think for yourself.

—Socrates

You now know where you are and your current position. The next step is to dwell deeper and understand you by assessing yourself as a person. While there are several parameters and ways to assess oneself, this section has focussed on three parameters that are of paramount importance. These include assessing your current strengths, knowledge, and present baseline. We will delve deeper into each of these parameters.

Two friends, Ted and Shane, met after several years. They decided to catch up over coffee at Starbucks for old times' sake. The aroma of the coffee made them nostalgic, reminding them about their childhood days. They sat down and spoke about their lives since they had last met. They discussed their achievements and how their children had grown. They were glad that they were both successful in their lives and caught up on their common friends.

As they were finishing their coffee, Shane complimented Ted about a certain glow Ted had on his face. It was a glow of contentment and fulfilment. So, in an envious tone, he asked Ted, "You seem to be content with life." Ted replied, "Yes, I am." He explained that ever since he knew where he was heading and his life purpose, he was less stressed about everything. He somehow felt energised whenever he sat down to understand how much he has progressed, knowing where he had started from. He reiterated, "The key is to know yourself and the journey you want to take in life." The conversation left Shane thinking that there was more to success than just materialistic achievements. He figured the key to happiness must be to know where you are, yourself, and where you want to be. Everything you then do will bring in more fulfilment and purpose to life.

To discover your life purpose, first you need to assess yourself holistically. This will allow you to understand where you want to go and how you will get there. Take some time to reflect while fearlessly assessing yourself.

Exercise:

1. Rate yourself across various facets of your life (financials, career, personal, health, family, and friends)
2. How would you rate your present health condition?
3. What is your current financial status?
4. How are your relationships at work, home, and with friends?
5. Are you happy with your present job or employer?
6. Are you content within the various aspects?
7. Are there any changes you want to bring about?
8. What do you wish your life to be?

Assess your current strength

In our pursuit of striving hard to grow and achieve more, we tend to be hard on ourselves. We often forget that we are humans and it is perfectly fine to be imperfect. More importantly, we need to constantly remind ourselves that we all have strengths that must be leveraged.

As a child, I remember a friend whose parents insisted that their child should write with the right hand when he was naturally left-handed. They went to the extent of engaging him for private writing tuitions. Gradually, he started to write with his right hand, much to his parent's delight. But he did not gain the speed required to complete his examination on time. He always fell short on completing his examination papers, and that affected his overall grades. On the flip side, he was a top cricket sportsman at school, and he did this batting with his left hand! Thinking back, he realised he would have scored higher marks in his examinations had his parents leveraged his natural strength of letting him write with his left hand.

If you are a natural salesperson and great in quickly establishing trust and relationships along with winning a client's confidence, that's your natural strength, and not writing software programs. If what you do brings you joy, then you must continue to pursue it while leveraging your strengths. You need to avoid self-criticism that suppresses your natural strengths and self-confidence.

Take a moment to list your top five strengths. Capture the strengths that first come to your mind, and do not stop if more strengths flow into your mind. This could be across various facets of life and could include your hobbies that you are pursuing. Your strengths could be communication, presentation, problem-solving, decision-making, investments, fast program coder, orator, pleasing personality, your smile, temperament, anything positive that comes to your mind.

Speak with your spouse, partner, family, and friends to validate your strengths. Accept their feedback gracefully with an open mind and without judging. You will be surprised by your list and the sudden rush of self-confidence. Imagine if a simple exercise like this can elevate your confidence, what magic could be performed if you leveraged your strengths.

Your core strength is doing what you are competent and capable of doing, while energising your passion with joy. Think of how you could apply these strengths to your daily life. Often, our self-criticism holds us back. It suppresses our inherent strengths and pushes them into a latent state. They must be regularly tapped and leveraged to progress. The secret to leveraging your strength is to maintain a success journal. These need not be big moments of glory. Capture the smaller wins; every little triumph should be logged and registered. The success journal will serve as your reservoir of positive reinforcement when you need it the most.

Exercise:

Step 1—Take a few minutes to write down your greatest successes in life. These could be across various aspects of your life like school, university, work, family, friends, financials, and hobbies, among others. Move to step 2 only after completing step 1.

Step 2—Against each of your successes, list down the skills and talents that helped you achieve them. As you reflect and recollect, do not limit the number of success stories that come to your mind. By the same token, do not limit the number of skills and talents that helped you achieve your successes in life. The skills and talents listed will form your repository of strengths.

No	My Success Story	Skills and Talents Used

Step 3—In the table below, list down your top five strengths from the previous exercise. Against each of these, identify how you will use these strengths to further your progress at work, home, relationship, financials, self-development, and more.

No	My Strengths (Skills and Talents)	Will Be Used For

Step 4—Identify the people that energise you, what do they energise you about, and identify the energy triggers and what happens next.

Step 5—Brainstorm with yourself how you could use more of these strengths in your personal and professional life. What opportunities do these strengths present to you in your life?

Assess your current knowledge

Ask a high school or college graduate this question. What per centage of their academic education do they apply in their day-to-day jobs? The answer is probably not much. Do not get me wrong. This in no way devalues or relegates our education system. Our education system helps us build the foundation of our knowledge repository. It builds the core value system and fundamental capabilities required to do the job. This educational foundation helps us get our first and subsequent jobs. While our education system will always remain the perpetual knowledge base, it is the incremental new knowledge and new skills which one acquires that will help them differentiate and succeed.

The pace of new customer demands is driving the pace of new technology development across industries, which in turn is driving the need to acquire new knowledge and skills. Yesterday's knowledge and skills will not suffice to grow in the new age world. The pace of new technology development is driven by automation, artificial intelligence, and data, which will give rise to new job profiles demanding new skills. The unprecedented pace of change in a knowledge economy means that only the smartest will survive, thrive, and lead the race. With the rapid change in technology and consumer habits and the disruptive impact of digitalisation across the horizon, the key to survival is assessing and building your knowledge repository. After all, we are now living in a knowledge economy, where the currency is data and the asset is your knowledge.

Exercise:

1. Rate yourself from one to ten on your present knowledge with respect to your job role/position, colleagues, and industry peers. This would provide a realistic assessment of your current position.
2. The next step is to identify what expertise you wish to acquire in the next three to six months. What new knowledge and skills do you need to bridge the gap. How do you plan to achieve these new levels? What are the sources of

gaining knowledge? They could be books, tutorials, trainings, social media platforms, or even information freely available on the web. You could upgrade your knowledge on the current and new developments impacting your industry, company, products, customers, suppliers, employees, and your role. These make great icebreakers in business meetings, which not only demonstrate your knowledge but also are great conversation starters that facilitate building relationships.

3. Establish your learning style. This could be reading, listening, or watching videos. Follow this with your knowledge acquisition list by ensuring you invest at least thirty minutes of your time every day to gaining new knowledge. That would amount to 3.5 learning hours a week or 14 learning hours a month or 168 learning hours a year. All this, at the very least, sharing the knowledge gained would have a compounding effect on its value.

Ascertain your baseline

People often say, "Pursue your dreams no matter what and when." It is true you should pursue your dreams, but make sure you have first built a robust safety net to take care of your basic sustenance levels. This is not to suggest delaying the pursuit of your dreams until you are financially sound. The baseline is the level below which one would never gamble in life. This is the minimum threshold level you always need to maintain to survive the realities of this world.

There are several stories of how people dropped out of school, started their business from their parents' garages or borrowed money from their friends to launch a small-scale start-up, and made it a million-dollar success overnight. While not discrediting these brilliant individuals for their success, the questions you need to ask yourself are: what is the probability that the worst case could happen to you and how prepared are you to sustain it? What people do not hear about are the stories of how individuals foolishly drowned themselves into financial bankruptcy. They over-leveraged themselves beyond their limits, and they borrowed money from people to pay off their old debts. In the process, they inherited more debts, and they went on until they could not sustain anymore. The problem with these people is that they did not know when to start or stop; they erratically jumped in without keeping aside money for the safety of their families and themselves. Their problems magnified when they did not apply common sense or had a contingency plan in place to get their lives back on track.

Every entrepreneur knows that while launching their business, they will encounter unplanned failures. They are mentally prepared to take them head-on and work supremely hard, and they persevere to bounce back again. They program themselves to be resilient and persistent to fight back and at most times make huge sacrifices to claw their way to success. These individuals have their contingency plans in case they fail. In either case, they tend to have a thousand-day plan to survive while launching their business. The contingency plan would factor in for their baseline or the level at which they break even to cover their basic costs.

Do a reality test and validate what would it take to pursue your dreams and at what costs—the keywords being "at what costs." What do you have to lose? This could include not just paying for your food, clothing, shelter, or anything else, but also the educational expenses for your children, mortgages and outgoing expenses. You need to work out your basic sustenance cost by month for a year.

Abraham Maslow captured the baseline needs beautifully in his Maslow's Hierarchy of Needs, where he states that people focus on Self-Actualisation and Self-Esteem only when they have achieved their lower levels of Belonging, Safety, and Physiological needs. The hungry stomach focusses on first filling the stomach and then pursuing dreams. You need to ensure you have your basic income or finances secured to provide for your basic daily needs, have a decent shelter to live in, and proper clothing to wear. Securing these baseline human needs will allow you to relentlessly focus and pursue larger dreams. Your minds will automatically develop an intense focus on the next level of Maslow's Hierarchy of Needs when you have secured the lower levels of need, which is your baseline.

The path to achieving your life purpose is an ongoing journey. It starts with assessing where you are today, where you want to be, and doing what you need to do while establishing your baseline as a fundamental step for survival. Your baseline is the core of your survival. Not securing your baseline is not only foolish but also suicidal. Start slow if you must and then work hard to make up for the lost time.

3.3 Manage Your FUD Factor— Manage Fear to Manage Your Uncertainty and Doubt

The big lesson in life, baby, is never be scared of anyone or anything.

—Frank Sinatra

We dare to dream; yet when we dream further, we are apprehensive of our dreams being realised. The uncertainty of achieving the dream makes us apprehensive. It makes the dream look unrealistic, and soon the dream drifts away—only to remain a dream. When we are inspired, we capture the energy from the ether and make it our own. We dream of the many things we want in our lives. We dream of making the first million dollars, starting a business, being a celebrity movie star or a sports person, buying a yacht, retiring early, or getting that senior position we wish to attain one day.

After dreaming for a while, we suddenly pause and think of our past and present. We think of the failures we had in the past and the barriers we are facing now. We allow our minds to drift and relive those failures and the downslide that came along with it. We begin to build an image in our minds of what went wrong and who all were responsible for it. We think of all our limitations that led to these failures. As we slide back further, our minds begin to decelerate from the earlier acceleration that came from the momentum of our dreams. A radical change takes over us, and we lose the confidence to pursue our dreams. We lose confidence in our abilities and the probability of our dreams happening. The mind stops dreaming about the future because we allowed it to be fed with our past unsuccessful experiences.

Nobody in their right senses plans to fail; they have only failed to plan. They either have a plan to succeed or may not have a plan at all. Some individuals and organisations fail, only to recover bigger and while some other individuals and organisations fail never to recover. They either stagnate into a slow death or never launch back from their failures.

Core attribute of failures

The core attribute around failures is "fear." First, fear to fail, and then fear to recover from a failure or to avoid another failure. This endless loop consumes one's confidence and freezes the brain and thought process from progressing. Fear, being parasitic in nature, rapidly grows depending on how much it is fed. The more apprehensive people are, the more fears feed into them. As people's fears grow larger, they avoid the initiatives and paths they need to take to follow their dreams and aspirations. Their fears become their roadblocks, get stronger, and take the centre stage in their lives.

The only failure is not to try.

—George Clooney

Fear works on the mind like a sickness. It first makes a small entry into the mind and then starts multiplying its way across the rest of the mind like a virus. The once-positive mind begins to turn negative. A negative mind reflects negatively on a person's behaviour, attitude, self-belief, self-esteem, and actions. This in time increases the person's stress levels and leads to degeneration of their mental and physical health conditions.

Fears are inherent in human beings and cannot be avoided. The Stone Age man used to fear attacks from wild animals and would have bonfires lit outside his cave to keep the wild animals away. Fears must be dismantled and then realigned to play a constructive role in your life. They need to be broken down bit by bit. This could take days, weeks, or even months depending on how deep-rooted your fear is. Past failures that had a large impact tend to create a deep-rooted fear within a person. The fear factor is influenced by the impact of your past failures. Fears are here to stay, and they form an integral part of our existence. It drives us to higher and higher levels of development, progress, and achievements. You need to let fear hold its constructive place in your life.

Fear is like an ingredient in a meal. It must be acknowledged and then blended with other ingredients like persistence, confidence, discipline, focus, resilience, common sense, and knowledge to gain productive progress. Similar to salt in a meal, it cannot be consumed on its own unless it is blended with all the other ingredients into the meal. Often, people get so overwhelmed by the fear factor that it ends up occupying the centre stage in their lives. Fear must be embraced with self-belief and self-confidence that they can be managed and leveraged as a source to drive higher performance levels.

Types of fears

What then are the different types of fears within us? According to Napoleon Hill in his bestseller book *The Law of Success*, there are six fears that prevent people from progressing in life. These are fear of poverty, fear of criticism, fear of ill health, fear of loss of love, fear of old age, and fear of death.

The first step is to identify the different types of fears within you and name each one of them. Write down the fears that come to your mind. Think deeper to understand the origin of these fears. Some fears will have an explained origin, while others will have an unexplained origin.

Write down everything you know about these fears and what you do not know. If the fear of financial loss is at the top of your mind, then create a table of what you own (assets) and the annual income you earn and what you owe (debts) and the annual expenses you incur. This simple exercise will let you know your current financial position as of the date and will clarify if the origin of your fear is explained or unexplained.

The process of listing and defining your fears will bring clarity and shed light on them. This is the first of many steps in overcoming your fears. You will begin to form a perspective of these fears and what they mean to you. You will begin to understand the impact of these fears and if they were imaginative or realistic.

Weeding off fears

Imagine your mind to be a garden in your house. You water the plants and the grass every day and do not let any weeds to grow in your garden. The moment you spot a weed growing, you uproot the weed and ensure it does not affect the other plants. Just as you protect your garden from the very first weed infecting the other plants, you must protect your mind from negative thoughts creeping in. Your mind, like your body, needs daily nourishment. You protect your body with clothes, nourish it with food, and take care of it by cleansing it daily. When you are unwell, you visit a doctor for medication and remedy. So why not nourish and look after your minds the same way you do for your body?

You must manage your mind to protect it from negative thoughts and past failures. The past is the past; there is nothing more to it except the learnings you have gained. It will not change the present or the future. You must live by being mindful of the present and focus on the future by leveraging the experiences gained.

Our thoughts and actions are limited by the saboteurs that reside within our minds. These saboteurs serve as limiting factors that hinder the path to following one's life purpose. They remind us of our failures and our incapability to move forward in the desired direction. Saboteurs come in various forms. At times they could be obvious, and at other times they could be hidden—camouflaged and deceptive. The key to managing saboteurs is to identify them and know they exist. They can either be consciously offloaded or left to silently exist within us. Some saboteurs are essential to driving us forward. Take the saboteur of self-criticism; if left unmanaged, it could leave you demoralised; and if managed, it could drive you to towards self-improvement.

To manage your uncertainties and doubts, first you need to manage your fears. Higher your fears, the higher will be your uncertainties and doubts. The uncertainties and doubts that creep into your minds are only but natural as you embark on a journey filled with new paths, crossroads, and new situations. Our ability to handle this is based on our attitudes, self-confidence, and perseverance. When these are lacking and we don't have the experience and competency, we begin to doubt ourselves and let the uncertainty of the situation overwhelm us.

Soichiro Honda attended an interview at the Toyota Motor Corporation, only to be rejected as unfit for the job. His aspirations and perseverance led him to design his own scooters at home, before he was encouraged by his family and friends to launch his business. Honda went on to revolutionise the two-wheeler industry before entering the automobile industry. **Thomas Edison** failed more than a thousand times and was thought to be stupid and a slow learner by his teacher. The same boy went on to invent the light bulb, after more than a thousand unsuccessful attempts.

Embracing fears gives us the permission to fail. Nobody wishes for failures, but when they do happen, we should be better prepared to learn, recover, and move on. Every successful individual or organisation has several failure stories behind their success. The secret has been their resilient character to experience this setback and bounce back from it—stronger. Yes, exactly. They do not have failure in their vocabulary, just temporary defeats, or moments of adversity. They believe this is nature's way of enlightening them. They delve into the learnings they have gained and investigate into the future on how they could apply this newfound wisdom.

More importantly, they move forward and then scale upward in their quest to follow their dreams. Their journey is filled with temporary setbacks; some of them anticipate well ahead of time, and some others spring up as surprises driven by the external world, not within their control. Each temporary defeat makes them stronger and wiser. They grow into strong, resilient characters driven by an unquenched thirst for persistence and discipline. Persistence to stay the course, no matter what, and discipline to do what is necessary to move them forward to their goals.

With every temporary setback, they pause to reflect and reconnect with their goals, and then realign their plans to execute and achieve their goals. Interestingly, the setbacks become fewer in number, and the recovery time becomes faster. Their minds become like a fortress fending off fears even before they are launched in their mind. They transform their fears of failure into a source of motivation. By embracing these fears, they make fears play a constructive role in their lives.

Fear of change

Fear of change is another big fear that hinders the progress of both individuals and organisations. It holds them back from dreaming, aspiring, and embracing their goals and missions. Fear of change is driven by many factors such as fear of the unknown, fear of failure, fear of instability, fear of rejection, and fear of incapability—all contributing to the destabilisation of the current status quo.

The ability of individuals and organisations to relaunch themselves with every failure has been one of the key factors contributing to their success. Embracing change helps individuals to transform and progress in their jobs, roles, skills, competency, and more. Relaunching time and again gets inborn into their newfound DNA, and over time, it becomes an integral part of their lives.

When we look back at some of the successful individuals and organisations and why they ceased to exist today, it is shocking to learn the commonality between the two. They refused to accept the reality of the situation, they refused to change and adapt, their past successes overshadowed their present perspective, and they refused to innovate and differentiate themselves.

We are living in a disruptive age, where change is the key to survival and innovation is the key to differentiation. Disruption has impacted industries in different forms. Some industries have experienced unprecedented changes in the landscape virtually overnight. While some other industries have offered the incumbent players an opportunity to adapt and respond. In either case, it has been the individuals who have taken the proactive step to adapt at varying points that have succeeded, and likewise, with organisations that thrived by staying connected with reality, by innovating, reinventing, differentiating, and driving higher levels of personalisation in their products and services.

To quote **President Franklin Roosevelt,** "The only thing we have to fear is fear itself." Fear originates and surfaces in various forms. These could be fear of death, rejection, ill health, failure, and other reasons. While there are several types of fears, interestingly, the fear of public speaking is among the top five fears individuals possess. The best orators know that the only way to overcome the fear of public speaking is to proactively prepare and thoroughly practice well in advance.

To truly assess yourself, you need to understand the fears, uncertainties, and doubts holding you back. Fears can be managed and responded to in several ways. It depends from person to person. Fear, Uncertainty, and Doubt (FUD) have many sources of origin but largely come from unpreparedness to face the situation. The mindsets leading to uncertainty about progressing are people's lack of knowledge, skills, and competency; or their lack of confidence and self-belief; or a combination of both.

Exercise:

Open your mind to assess your fears. Ask yourself these questions and note down the responses that come to your mind.

1. List down all your fears.
2. Categorise them into health, personal, finances, family, etc.
3. What could be the worst that could happen to you with each of the above fears?
4. Is it something you could proactively avoid? If your answer is no, then what are your alternatives?
5. If your answer is yes, write down the steps you will take to proactively manage them.
6. Is there a new opportunity for you in this and what is it?
7. Who could help you recover?
8. What knowledge and skills do you need to proactively onboard?
9. What types of resources would you need to bounce back?
10. Are these fears blocking you from pursuing your dreams and life purpose?

Now that you know what fears are and how to manage them, how does that make you feel? Bring it on! That is right! You should embrace your fears to master and manage them, else they will end up controlling your life. Appreciate and accept them like a new friend. In time, you will master the art of managing your fears, both proactively and reactively.

3.4 Find Your Life Purpose

*To begin to think with purpose is to enter the
ranks of those strong ones who only recognise
failure as one of the pathways to attainment.*

—James Allen

Having gone through the earlier part of the Assess phase sections, you are now prepared for the most important part of the Assess phase. It is about finding your life purpose and committing to it. One of the greatest gifts you can give yourself is the joy of having a life purpose.

How often do we see people around us who lack energy, motivation, and a sense of direction in their lives? They have surrendered to their status quo, like a rudderless boat, to the currents of ocean waves. Moving in any direction is fine with them. They continue to remain oblivious to their outside world, while remaining insensitive to their inner world. They hand over their future to fate, doing nothing about it themselves. Their inner world keeps calling them through various opportunities in their lives, but their deafness to listen to their inner voice leaves them in this rudderless state. You may have come across such people—and even you may have been in these situations in the past or at present. These are good people with good intentions but unfortunately they lack a sense of purpose in their lives.

We are all born for a purpose

The purpose of our lives is to be happy.

—Dalai Lama

You are born with a life purpose that is unique to you and resides dormant within you. It is waiting to be released like a genie in a bottle. You only need to pause, reflect, and listen to your inner voice—the voice that always seems to guide and talk to you. You are naturally resourceful, and the path to unlocking your problems will naturally unfold in your minds. The only roadblocks are the ones placed in your mind. Once these roadblocks are kept aside or removed, ideas and solutions flow into the mind. You need to give yourself the time to identify your life purpose, acknowledge it, and honour it. Having a clear life purpose is the fuel to remain in a high state of energy. Your actions will resonate at a stronger frequency with your life purpose, thereby supporting/guiding the path towards achieving your goals.

On identifying your life purpose, your inner system will automatically get recalibrated for high performance. You will have a deep sense of purpose in life, and this will be reflected in the way you think, walk, talk, engage with people, and believe in yourself. Higher the resonance with your life purpose, the higher will be your commitment and chances to succeed. You will be energised and motivated in new ways that you have never witnessed before. Work becomes a pleasure; you will sleep well with a sense of fulfilment, knowing what you need to do the next day. The next morning, you wake up with a sense of direction and purpose.

You subconsciously know what needs to be done next to get you closer to your life purpose.

The human body is unique, in that it needs to continuously know its current position and have a clear direction of its next end destination. We are programmed to work with clarity of purpose. When this does not exist, we either follow someone else's directions or our systems consume higher energy levels doing tasks that do not energise us. When we have a purpose, we attract undiscovered energy levels, thereby achieving more with less. That is the power of having a life purpose. The challenge people face is not having a life purpose, but not taking the initiative and time to find their life purpose.

With your life purpose firmly placed in your mind, you gain the momentum to embark on your journey. Momentum is precious once in motion; you should work to retain the momentum into continuous motion. The efforts required to retain the momentum in motion are far lesser than the efforts required to start the momentum. Think of the efforts required to set a wheel into motion. The initial effort is significantly higher than the intermediate effort required to keep it in motion.

So how does one find their life purpose?
Finding your life purpose demands that you pause what you are doing. Pause to take a breather and check in on yourself to know where you are headed. You need to reflect on what makes you happy, what do you love doing the most, and what comes naturally and joyfully to you. You are naturally inclined to a passion that is unique to you, and only you can find it. You may

feel you are naturally inclined to music, sports, cooking, travelling, writing, or even robotics. This needs to resonate and energise you instantaneously. If it is cooking, delve in deeper to understand what it is that you like about cooking. This could be pursuing your career as a chef, opening a restaurant, contracting for a new food franchise, publishing a cookbook, opening your own cloud kitchen, and more.

You will enjoy this journey rather than being pushed into it. You need to follow this by identifying the activities that you love and expressing the joy it brings to you. This would be at the top of your mind. Identify the values (care, love, respect, being relevant, etc.) that resonate within you. This is crucial as you inch closer to establishing your life purpose statement. Knowing your values will help you derive and validate your life purpose.

Knowing your life purpose will allow you to not only identify where you want to go but also reaffirm your target destination. As you progress in your journey, your life purpose must be refined at regular intervals or even changed depending on your circumstances and situations. It either gets reinforced with more depth or tends to change completely when the original life purpose has been achieved. If you do not know your life purpose, do not stress over it. Take your time to discover it. Respond to the below questions to help you find or validate your life purpose. This is a preliminary list to get you progressing. The subsequent chapters will answer the question: "How will you reach your end destination?"

Exercise:

Take thirty minutes either early in the morning or at night to answer these questions. Make sure you are in a quiet place without any distractions. You owe this to yourself. Do not judge your responses to the questions; just write them down as they naturally flow out from your mind. Once completed, you can go back and refine or rephrase your answers to bring in greater clarity.

This exercise may require that you spend more time with yourself to complete the exercise. As your mind progressively reflects, you will gain better clarity of yourself, thereby taking you closer to your life purpose.

Questions to Help You Discover Your Life Purpose:

Questions	Responses
1. What makes me come alive?	
2. What am I passionate about?	
3. What issues are holding me back?	
4. What are my personal goals?	
5. What are my professional goals?	
6. What am I trying to achieve?	
7. What does success look like to me?	
8. What does happiness look like to me?	
9. What keeps me awake at night?	
10. What activities energise me?	
11. What activities or moments make me feel acknowledged and loved?	
12. What are my learnings from past challenges I have overcome?	

13. If I had all the resources in the world with no limitations, what would my life look like?	
14. What legacy do I want to leave behind? What do I want to leave behind for future generations?	
15. What are the values that I live by?	
16. Write down five words that would characterise me.	
17. What kind of situations makes me feel relevant and important?	
18. What makes me stand out from the crowd?	
19. Where do I add the greatest value?	
20. What problems am I good at solving?	
21. How will I measure my life?	
22. What do I want my life to be about?	
23. Knowing what I now know, what will I do differently?	
24. What actions will I take to pursue my journey towards my life purpose?	
25. What makes me unique?	

Questions to Progress Forward

1. What opportunities lie ahead of me?	
2. What strengths can I leverage?	
3. What skills and competency would I need?	
4. Who are the people who can support me?	
5. What resources would I need?	

Key definite aim—your personal mission statement

Take time to write down your key definite aim, which is your personal mission statement, keeping aside all and any limitations that come to your mind. For instance, my current key definite aim is "I am the lighthouse that brings direction and joy to people in their work and personal lives." Write your key definite aim below. This is something that instantaneously resonates with you every day and every moment. It should energise you, lift your spirits, and immediately bring you happiness.

> My purpose in life is . . .

Schedule a thirty-minute monthly appointment with yourself to review your personal mission statement. This is your opportunity to revalidate, reinforce, and renew your personal mission statement. Your mission statement will change with your aspirations, circumstances, and goals.

3.5 Tools to Assess

There are several tools that can help assess your present situation. Some of the relevant tools have been listed below.

1. **Wheel of Life** (WoL): Take fifteen minutes to do a WoL assessment. There are various sources that will provide you with a WoL template. Below is a simple WoL.
   a. Using the WoL template, assign scores to yourself across the various aspects of your life. This includes health, family, physical environment, personal growth, fun/recreation, social life, and career. This is your present/current state.
   b. The next step is to identify one or two aspects of your life where you wish to see an improvement today. Think of what the improvements would look like for you.
   c. Now using a different colour or marker, write down your new wish ratings. This will be your future state. If it is health improvement, your future state could be to reduce weight by 5 kg in three months or running a 10-km race in six months. If it is professional career, it could be changing your role or job in the next twelve months; if it's family, it could be spending an additional hour every day with your family.

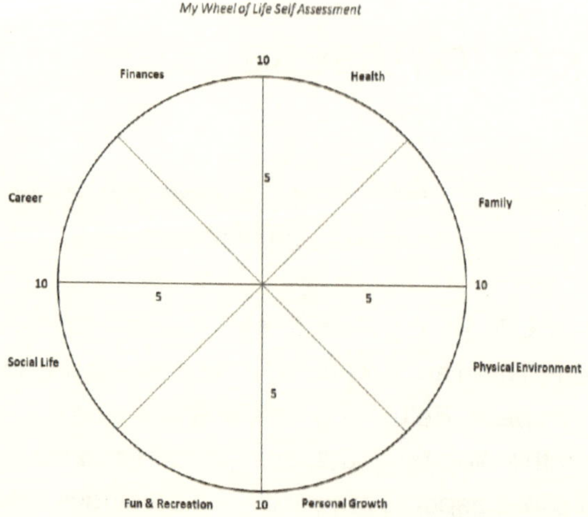

2. **Nine-Box Grid Model:** Knowing what you now know about your performance and your potential as an individual, how do you map the two to know your current position and then target where you want to be? The answer to this question is addressed by the **Nine-Box Grid Model.** This model is widely used by organisations to identify the top performers and high-potential performers. Individuals can also use it to assess themselves and align with where they need to be. This alignment must be with your life purpose and core strengths.

    As an exercise, rate yourself on your past/current performance (Y-axis) versus your current potential (X-axis). The grid has predefined nine boxes that will help you know in which box you currently belong.

    Knowing your current intersection point or box, your next task is to identify and align into which of the nine boxes you plan to progress. Work out the improvement plan and how this plan would be achieved. The nine boxes are depicted in the table below.

High Performance	Trusted Professional	Strong Performer	Top Talent
Moderate Performance	Skilled	Core Performer	Strong Potential
Low Performance	Watch List	Weak Performer	Emerging Star
Nine-Box Grid	Low Potential	Moderate Potential	High Potential

3. **Pareto Principle:** The Pareto principle (also known as the 80/20 rule or the law of the vital few states that, for many events, roughly 80 per cent of the effects come from 20 per cent of the causes. Management consultant Joseph M. Juran suggested the principle and named it after Italian economist Vilfredo Pareto, who noted the 80/20 connection while at the University of Lausanne in 1896, as published in his first work: *Cours d'économie politique*. In it, Pareto showed that approximately 80 per cent of the land in Italy was owned by 20 per cent of the population.

List down all your activities, twenty-four hours of the day, for the next thirty days. Capture the time you sleep, exercise, socialise, work, etc. Once these activities have been captured, the data will provide you with a near-accurate analysis that 20 per cent of your activities are contributing to 80 per cent of your productivity.

Reflect on your life purpose and goals to gain a deeper understanding of the relevance of these 20 per cent activities and to determine what must be done next to achieve your goals. These 20 per cent activities may need more time allocated in your day or might need to be dropped or replaced with another constructive activity or may even be done at a different time of the day.

4. **PESTLE Analysis**

The PESTLE tool:

It is used by organisations to help identify factors affecting their business environment. This powerful tool can also be applied to individuals. The six factors in the PESTLE tool include Political, Economic, Social, Technology, Legal, and Environmental. The six factors are self-explanatory and should be applied with common sense.

Individuals may find that while applying this tool, some factors may or may not be relevant. That is perfectly fine, as this is a momentary assessment; it could be relevant at a later stage. For instance, if you have received an employment opportunity to relocate to a new place with a new company, all the six factors will come into play. Compare this to getting a promotion within the same company and the same location.

Applying PESTLE would give a structure to research or assess the external factors that must be considered before relocating to the new job or new role. For instance, providing you with an insight into the impact of new industry trends that could impact your existing role or job; Or an insight to understand which industries and companies have a high potential for growth that could be your prospective employers; or the potential to launch a new business in that specific industry.

5. **SWOT Analysis**: Do a Strengths, Weaknesses, Opportunities, and Threats Analysis. SWOT analysis was invented in the 1960s by a management consultant named Albert Humphrey at the Stanford Research Institute.

    - Using the below template, list down all your strengths. Write down everything that comes to your mind. Do not judge yourself, just do a brain dump of every little thing that you believe could be your strength, even if it is small.
    - Next, think of all the opportunities that lie ahead of you. Think of opportunities at home, with family, friends, work, within your industry, and among competitors, suppliers, and others.
    - Identify the strengths that could be leveraged for the opportunities that lie ahead of you.
    - List down the threats that you need to be aware of, which could hinder your progress. Being aware of the threats will subconsciously shift your mind to proactively being prepared should you encounter one of these threats.

My SWOT

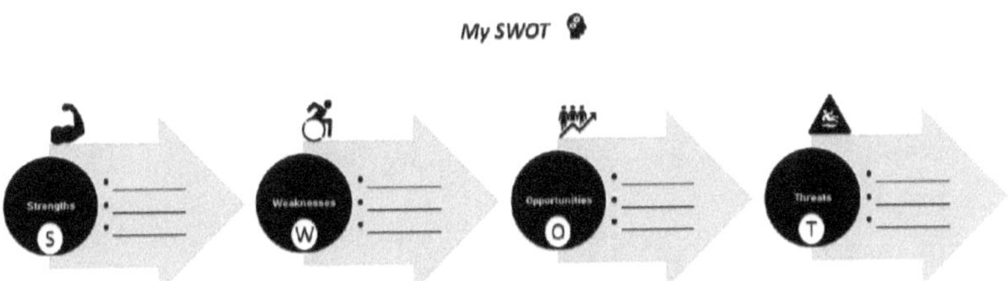

After having captured your Strengths, Opportunities, and Threats, list down your areas of improvement. These are traditionally called Weaknesses. Weaknesses are purposefully captured last to allow the mind to focus on the opportunities that lie ahead, by leveraging the strengths and being aware of the external dangers or threats.

Chapter Four

Phase 2 — Align

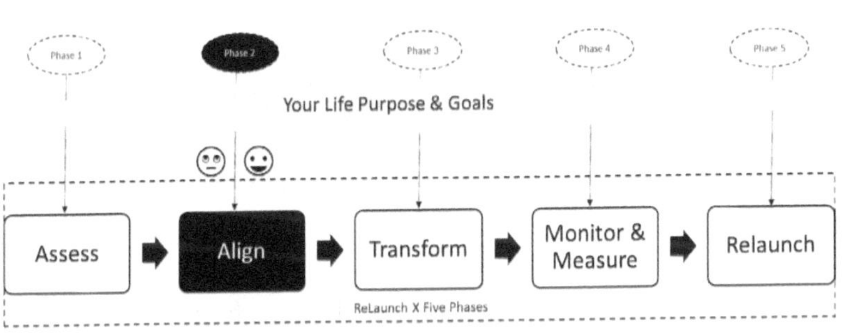

*Any definite chief aim that is deliberately fixed
in mind and held there, with the determination
to realise it, finally saturates the subconscious
mind until it automatically influences the physical
action of the body toward the attainment of that
purpose.*

—*Napoleon Hill, The Laws of Success*

Congratulations! You have completed the foundation step to relaunching yourself. In the Assess phase, you successfully established your current coordinates, gained a deeper understanding and appreciation for fears, and importantly identified your life purpose. You are beginning to gain a sense of control knowing your life purpose and getting a deeper understanding of your fears and how to manage them.

Knowing your life purpose is the fundamental building block to self-mastery and transformation. If you have not completed the exercise to determine your life purpose, take the time to identify your life purpose that best resonates with you now. Your life purpose will change over time as you gain deeper insights and clarity about yourself.

Having completed the Assess phase, you now need to build alignment of your actions with your end destination and your goals. In this phase, we will cover actions that will help you understand how to build alignment with your life purpose.

4.1 Establish Your Goals

If you can tune into your purpose and really align with it, setting goals so that your vision is an expression of that purpose, then life flows much more easily.

—Jack Canfield

Successful archers take a few moments to look at their target before going through their eleven archery steps. They focus their eyes on the highest scoring area, take a few deep breaths, and first visualise hitting the target in their mind before releasing the arrow. Once they are mentally prepared, they go through their archery motion from taking their *stance* to *release* and *follow through*. This three-step motion is repeatedly practiced in their minds and then in reality. They know their goals and what they must do to hit the high scoring targets.

Like the archer, you must go through the goal-setting process on how to visualise your long-, mid-, and short-term goals. Your goals, once written down, get automatically locked into your inner systems, and your focus shifts to execution. You then rehearse in your mind how you will meet your goals.

Have you experienced some days when you took the time to prepare a To-Do list and later had the pleasure of striking off each completed task? The daily tasks you completed, helped you reach closer to accomplishing your goals. This in turn gave you a sense of purpose and fulfilment. It energised you in a magical way that motivated you to higher levels of performance. This is the power of establishing goals.

We would have come across start-up companies that had a great idea but only to go bust in a few months. These start-ups got off the block swiftly but lacked clear goals and plans to back up their ideas. Their ideas got fuzzier and lost appeal, and their momentum slowed down, even before they could launch.

This is no different for organisations that launch their products and services into a new market without knowing what their goals are, what they want to achieve, and how they will measure their efforts. Without clear short-, mid-, and long-term goals, they are unlikely to have a successful market launch.

Companies that have established their goals have been more successful. They are wired uniquely and focus all their energies to complete their tasks and achieve their goals predictably. For instance, their first-year goal could be to establish the brand and win 1 per cent market share at a specific price, profitability, and product category. Their three-year goal could be to increase their market share to 2 per cent with emerging dominance in specific industries. Their five-year goal could be to have 5 per cent of the market share and be among the top five players in their ecosystem, serving the top 20 per cent of customers who matter the most.

Steps to setting goals
The foundation to setting goals is to link them to your life purpose and values. Goals can be set by adopting an *Integrated Goal Plan*

(IGP). The IGP will ensure that goals are built on top of each other, making them progressive in nature. The progressive goals are built in a step-like fashion, taking you to the next level, only on completion of the previous-level goals. This incremental approach brings in the power of breaking down your tasks for the overall achievements of your goals.

Exercise:

Your *IGP* can be established by following the below steps:

1. Establish your life purpose and values.

2. List down all your goals in alignment with your life purpose.

3. Segregate them into the below three categories:
   a. Long Term: Five years and three years,
   b. Mid Term: Twelve and six months,
   c. Short Term: Three months, one month, fortnight, and one week.

4. Next, prioritise your goals in each category.

5. Based on your short-term goals, outline your daily *Tasks-To-Do.*

6. Once your Tasks-To-Do is prepared, segregate the tasks into categories A, B, and C.
   a. Category A includes *urgent/important* tasks and *must* be done today or during the week without fail.

    b. Category B includes *not urgent/important* tasks and *should* be done proactively during the week or month, else they would become urgent.

    c. Category C includes *urgent/not important* tasks and *need* to be done during the week, but only after addressing categories A and B tasks.

7. Focus on working through the urgent and important tasks when your energy levels are high. These are tasks that were earlier *not urgent/important* and have now become *urgent/important* for you, thereby shifting your position from being proactive to reactive.

8. You must ensure at least 20 per cent of your time every week is allocated to *not urgent/important* tasks.

9. Completion of your daily tasks will take you incrementally closer to your overall goals.

   At the end of each day, follow the daily ritual of reflecting for five minutes. Write down your next day's *Tasks-To-Do* before you go to sleep at night.

10. Start each day by first glancing at your *Tasks-To-Do* and then visualising how you want your next day to unfold.

Do not be dejected if you do not complete your *Tasks-To-Do* as planned. After all, we are humans, and it is perfectly fine to improve with time. Carry the incomplete list forward to the next day with a new set of updated tasks. Do not be hard on yourself; rather, be persistent to complete the category A tasks list followed by the categories B and C tasks list.

Follow the ritual of reflection

Reflection is a form of mediation; when followed with discipline, it becomes a ritual. It gives you an insight into what needs to be done and helps to drive continuous improvement and reach your goals.

1. Invest ten minutes, every weekend, to reflect on your week gone by and update your top five goals for the week and the fortnight.
2. On the last day of every month spend fifteen minutes to reflect on the whole month and update your top five goals for the month, including your three-, six-, and twelve-month goals.
3. As you undergo this monthly exercise, keep a close watch on your three- to five-year goals. Over time, this gets engraved deep into your mind.

My chief goal

Before you start, identify the one goal that, if achieved, would have the highest positive impact on your life. This is your main goal or chief goal. The chief goal is also referred to as the life purpose or chief definite aim in life as Napoleon Hill termed it. Review your goals, and you will realise that all your other goals are aligned to the achievement of your chief goal.

Complete the below goal-setting template to establish your goals across timelines.

My Chief Goal

The below table will help you to capture your long-, mid-, and short-term goals. The five-year goal should resonate with your life purpose. The short-term, one-year, and three-year goals should build on top of each other with the sole purpose of helping you achieve your five-year goal and fulfiling your life purpose.

Five-Year Goals

My goals	What are my key Tasks-To-Do	How will I achieve my goal	By when	Who can help me
List Your Goal				
List Your Goal				
List Your Goal				
List Your Goal				
List Your Goal				

The table below explains each attribute of the goal-setting template.

My goal	The goal you want to achieve in life now
What is my key Tasks-To-Do	What specific action will you take to achieve your goal
How will I achieve my goal	How will you go about completing the task
By when	Completion date for the task
Who can help me	Who within your network can support you in ensuring your task is completed

Three-Year Goals

My goals	What are my key Tasks-To-Do	How will I achieve my goal	By when	Who can help me
List Your Goal				
List Your Goal				
List Your Goal				
List Your Goal				
List Your Goal				

One-Year Goals

My goals	What are my key Tasks-To-Do	How will I achieve my goal	By when	Who can help me
List Your Goal				
List Your Goal				
List Your Goal				
List Your Goal				
List Your Goal				

Six-Month Goals

My goals	What are my key Tasks-To-Do	How will I achieve my goal	By when	Who can help me
List Your Goal				
List Your Goal				
List Your Goal				
List Your Goal				
List Your Goal				

Three-Month Goals

My goals	What are my key Tasks-To-Do	How will I achieve my goal	By When	Who can help me
List Your Goal				
List Your Goal				
List Your Goal				
List Your Goal				
List Your Goal				

One-Month Goals

My Goals	What are my key Tasks-To-Do	How will I achieve my goal	By when	Who can help me
List Your Goal				
List Your Goal				
List Your Goal				
List Your Goal				
List Your Goal				

Biweekly Goals

My goals	What are my key Tasks-To-Do	How will I achieve my goal	By when	Who can help me
List Your Goal				
List Your Goal				
List Your Goal				
List Your Goal				
List Your Goal				

Weekly Goals

My goals	What are my key Tasks-To-Do	How will I achieve my goal	By when	Who can help me
List Your Goal				
List Your Goal				
List Your Goal				
List Your Goal				
List Your Goal				

Daily Tasks-To-Do

What are my key Tasks-To-Do	How will I achieve my goal	By when	Who can help me	Priority (A/B/C)

Holistic approach and types of goals

Now that you know how to set goals using the Integrated Goal Plan (IGP), let us look at the different types of goals to provide a balanced approach to your life. There are various types of goals, but the most fundamental types *are personal, financial, family, health, and professional goals.* While we focus on these goals, it is important to know there are several types of other goals such as academic, knowledge, social, spiritual, and more.

Personal goals are core to an individual and usually focus on self-accomplishment, self-fulfilment, and self-improvement. They form the nerve centre around the other types of goals. Achieving personal goals usually has a ripple effect on achieving other goals.

Pio had a personal goal of visiting the Seven Wonders of the World before his fortieth birthday. He realised that he had visited three of the Seven Wonders of the World and was yet to see the Taj Mahal and the remaining wonders of the world. Being a person of Indian origin, he was embarrassed about not visiting the Taj Mahal. He made a commitment to himself to not only visit the Taj Mahal but also visit the remaining Seven Wonders of the World within the next three years.

To achieve his goal, he had to save some money, and this became one of his financial goals. He knew that to achieve his financial goals he would have to amend his lifestyle. He had to cut down on his weekend indulgence including dining at some of the expensive places. The money he saved every week was deposited into his savings account. He shifted his weekend activities to improving his fitness levels while eating healthy at home. This became his health goal. This change in lifestyle not only improved his health and fitness level but also allowed him to save money for his travel plans.

Within the first nine months, he saved enough money to visit the Taj Mahal, and this motivated him to save more. He successfully visited the remaining wonders of the world in the next two years, way before the three years' timeline he had set for himself. In the process, he achieved several of his goals, giving him an overall sense of fulfilment.

Professional goals and their dual impact

While all goals are important to individuals, professional goals impact both personal and work life. Professional goals are broadly divided into two categories. The first category is the individual's career aspirations and the goals they set for themselves. The second category consists of the goals that organisations set for their employees and their expectations from the employee. As an entrepreneur, if you run a successful company, it will reflect positively on your domestic goals and how you engage at home with your family and friends (dual impact). The same applies if you are excelling in your professional career and are on a fast track with a fancy title; the undiscovered confidence would carry on to your personal goals and life. You are likely to be more courageous and ambitious in your other goals. On the contrary, if you are not settled at your workplace, you are likely to be more conservative with your personal goals and frugal in your spending (dual impact).

Organisations are more complex than individuals. Complex because it requires not only setting individual goals but also building an alignment between the organisation's goals and the individual goals. This gets complex when the alignment involves thousands of employees, business units, and geographies.

Goals have a pivotal role in the growth of any organisation. They help the company to be aligned to its vision, mission, and core values. They guide the company to grow its revenues and market share, differentiate and remain competitive, and offer products and services of the highest level while delivering optimal customer service.

Establishing goals across the organisation is a fundamental ingredient to the successful functioning of any organisation. Most organisations have a mature system for setting, establishing, and measuring goals. They set clear goals and key result areas for their employees. They take into consideration the employees' academics, experience, competency, skills, aptitude, aspirations, potential, and more. Successful organisations work towards building resonance between the organisation's and individual's goals. They address the gaps that may cause dissonance with an individual and outline how the short- and mid-term goals would feed into their long-term goals. Successful organisations go a step further by investing in a learning and development plan for their employees. This works magically for all concerned towards achieving their goals.

SMART and cascading goals

While there are many ways to set goals, the most used models are *SMART and Cascading Model*. SMART when expanded is Specific, Measurable, Achievable, Relevant, and Time Bound. The criteria are commonly attributed to Peter Drucker's Management by Objectives concept.

What should your goal look like? In a word, your goals should be **SMART**

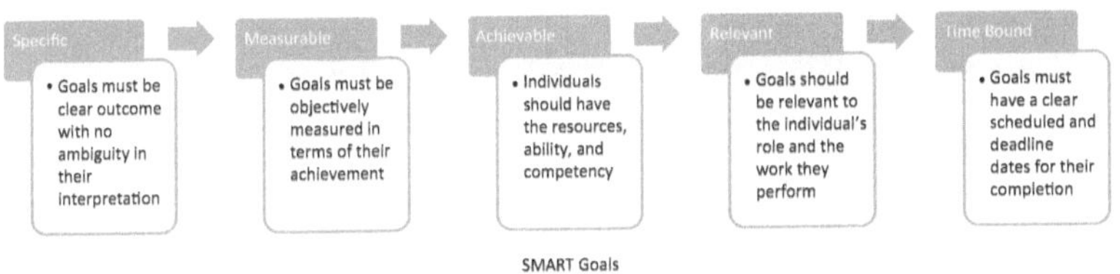

SMART Goals

Your goals should be specific and not generic or vague. If your financial goal is to be rich, it is a dream or a wish. A SMART financial goal would be to accumulate $1 million by the age of forty.

Specific goals eliminate vagueness and bring clarity. When a goal is specific, it allows the mind to form a clear image in your head. For instance, your work goal could be to achieve 150 per cent of your budget with a customer Net Promoter Score (NPS) of 9 in the current financial year, thereby making you eligible for a promotion. Your health goal could be to work out 45 minutes a day, five times a week, eat twice a day, and reduce 5 kgs in three months.

For instance, parents want to improve their child's performance at school. Is this a specific goal for the child? Not at all, as the child does not know what he/she must specifically achieve, and neither do the parents have a specific goal against which they can measure their child's progress. But if the goal is made specific, to achieve over 75 per cent for all subjects in the child's next midterm, then the probability of the child achieving the goal is high. Goals that are SMART become visible to the mind and are achieved.

Dr. Edwin Locke and Dr. Gary Latham invested many years exploring and researching on the Theory of Goal Setting. Dr. Locke concluded that 90 per cent of the time, goals that were specific, challenging, and time bound led to a relatively higher performance from employees. Interestingly, they also found that working towards clear goals was highly motivating for employees, which in turn improved their performances. This ultimately evolved into the SMART goal-setting model. In 1990, Dr. Edwin Locke and Dr. Gary Latham published their work *A Theory of Goal Setting and Task Performance*. They outlined five goal-setting principles that improve the success ratio of achieving our goals. The five principles are Clarity, Challenge, Commitment, Feedback, and Task Complexity.

While all five principles are equally important, "challenge" and "commitment" stand out. When challenging goals are set, they seamlessly motivate individuals. Goals should not be so challenging that they cannot be achieved or so simple that they do not challenge the individual to push hard towards attaining the goal. Achieving SMART goals leads to acknowledgement, recognition, and higher self-esteem. Think about the time when you achieved your annual sales targets in nine months or when you completed your project ahead of schedule or you onboarded your first investor in the first year of your start-up's operations.

The other commonly adopted model for setting goals is **Cascading**. In this model, the goals cascade down by getting deconstructed and aligned from one level of the organisation to the next level. Goals can be cascaded down across multiple levels from business, division, department, team, and individual goals. Leaders at each level work towards building alignment with their teams while ensuring that the goals are challenging and achievable.

On thinking big with goals

Having read the book *The Magic of Thinking Big* by David J. Schwartz, I am often reminded "Think Big to Achieve Big." In one of my tenures with a global multinational company, we grew revenues twenty times over five years by thinking big to achieve big. Once we committed to the annual revenue and profitability targets, we called out what needed to be done and how we had planned to achieve it. I recollect the words of wisdom from a senior colleague who reminded us "Think big to plan big and achieve big, but remember execution is everything."

I would go about my "thinking big to achieve big" mantra by constantly reminding myself every day. I would start by writing down my annual revenue and profitability targets (with a 25 per cent uplift) on multiple post-its and stick them on my desk, laptop, telephone, mirror, car dashboard, and even on my study table at home. This served as a constant reminder of the targets I needed to overachieve. My mind would subconsciously work at all times, even when I was asleep, on how this target would be overachieved, who would be able to support me, which products and services offered the most value, which customers offered the highest potential, and which team members would play a pivotal role in this journey. I would narrow down on the potential big deals that would make a difference and ensured we won at least one-third of them.

My *think big to achieve big* mindset would then rub off on to the team. The team worked as a single unit to effortlessly build and gain the mindshare of the relevant stakeholders. The stakeholders would include clients, partners, internal presales, and management. We would unearth new business challenges and needs from our clients. Over time, we innovated, made strategies, and invested efforts to find solutions to meet these business challenges and needs. This helped us grow the revenue pipeline, target the mega deals, venture into new offerings, and forge new alliances and partnerships. In the process, we effortlessly raised our performance levels. We did this consistently for several years; so much so, it became a way of life. We branded ourselves as the *alpha* performers who would stay focussed, relentlessly collaborate with an *all win* attitude, make the necessary sacrifices, and persist until we collectively overachieved our targets.

Alpha performers know what they want, how they are going to get it, who will support them in achieving their goals, and their approach resonates positively with their ecosystem. This positivity not only motivated the team and improved their performances but also enabled them to earn more and enhance their careers.

We started each year believing we would achieve our targets for the year, yet anxious about how we would manage the external market factors. By mid-year, we were well and truly on track to achieve our annual targets, giving us the necessary boost to focus on overachieving our annual targets. This was truly a magical growth experience we witnessed year-on-year. Our business goals were always challenging, and this made it exciting as we needed to think out of the box to overcome all hurdles and consistently grow.

Challenging goals resonate with the team, and a natural force of commitment evolves. This natural force progressively gets stronger. Organisations gain their employees' commitment by not only involving them early on in the goal-setting process but also by being transparent that the goals can be realistically achieved and are in alignment with the company's strategic objectives.

4.2 Understand Your Points of Inflection

The whole secret of a successful life is to find out what is one's destiny to do, and then do it.

—Henry Ford

Many years ago, early on in my career, a senior colleague shared with me that there was no straight path to achieving your goals. The path has multiple turns, bends, and ups and downs, backed by a plan and an undeterred commitment to achieving your goals. Each change of direction to your path is called the *Point of Inflection*, a point when you change your course in pursuit of progressing towards your goal.

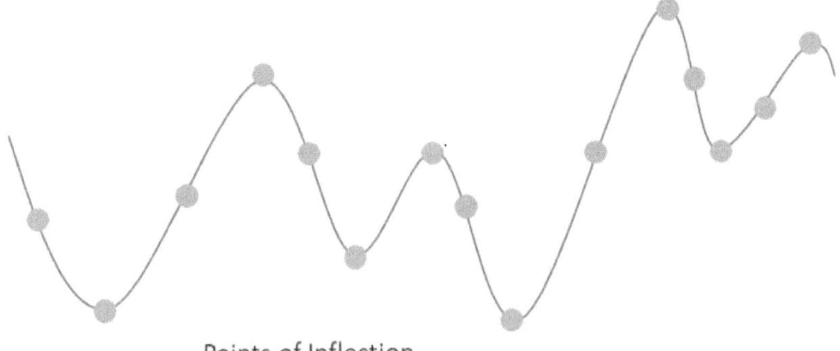

Points of Inflection

Plans end up being theoretical if they are not regularly validated and updated. The action plan may require taking one or more steps back, or to the side or forward, to overcome their immediate hurdles and move one step closer to their goals. It is like a game of football where each player passes the ball forward, sideward, or even backward to retain control of the game and progress towards scoring a goal against their opposition.

The *points of inflection* demand that you continuously and innovatively think on your feet and think "what next" while keeping a focussed watch on progressing towards your goal. You work with your plan while constantly adopting new tactics to stay on course to achieve your goals. It demands that you proactively modify your actions based on your situation and do what is required to progress towards your goals.

Our lives, like the ocean waves, go through highs and lows. While staying focussed on your goals, you must be able to sense and predict when you are approaching the next high or low. This may not be easy at first, but with practice, you will become mindful of your progress and can foresee what lies ahead. More importantly, you will begin to sharpen your instincts to adapt and act according to your surroundings.

On the one hand, the challenges for being on the rise of a wave are to sustain and consistently perform to retain the upward momentum. On the other hand, the challenges for being on the fall of the wave are to decelerate the fall, take stock, rework the plans, and take corrective actions (your point of inflection) towards an upward trajectory.

Both individuals and organisations must anticipate their inflection points in their journey towards achieving their goals and swiftly recalibrate their course when they reach their point of inflection. Anticipating this change in direction, backed by execution, is what enables individuals and organisations to differentiate themselves and progress forward. Our ability to predict and prepare in advance for the next inflection point is what will differentiate us from the rest.

Inflection points for individuals

Inflection points are driven by internal and external factors. For individuals allowing themselves to slip into a state of obsolescence, without moving to the next inflection point, is like taking a slow death pill. They need to continuously acquire new knowledge, skills, and competencies to stay relevant to the ecosystem. They need to change and adapt to the new work environment, a new profile of customers, and be attuned to the new way of life. On reaching your inflection point, the key to progress is embracing change and willingness to adapt.

Individuals who embraced their status quo with a deep refusal to change, at their inflection point, have become irrelevant! They have either been pushed into early retirement or have moved into a state of obsolescence. Individuals who have refused to continuously gain new knowledge; build new skills; change the way they engage at work; and adapt to new information, technology, and operational systems have been left behind.

The era of digitalisation has changed the way people shop, buy, and consume products and services. While the degree of digitalisation may vary from country to country or from industry to industry, it has now become the new normal. The COVID-19 pandemic has accelerated the adoption of digitalisation. This new normal has brought tremendous disruption across the ecosystem including buyers, sellers, employees, and employers. Higher disruption leads to more change. The rapid pace of change leads to higher points of inflection, thereby forcing individuals to frequently adapt to change.

The younger generation and the more resilient older generation have been quick to adapt to the new normal or ecosystem. They have adopted a curious approach to understanding what is going on around them not only in their work life but also in their personal lives. They have understood the dynamism of the new economy, which brought with it the gigantic waves of disruptions. They have crossed multiple points of inflection while adapting to new changes that came along the way.

Inflection points for organisations
For organisations, the new economy has brought about its own sets of unique challenges. Some companies have invested millions of dollars trying to understand the past and present, while remaining paralytic to take concrete actions on their future. There are other companies, both incumbents as well as start-ups, who have taken a nimble-footed approach in moving fast and failing fast, only to learn, relaunch quickly, and win big swiftly.

They have anticipated that in the new economy it would be difficult to predict the inflection points and hence have committed to remain in the state of continuous improvement backed by innovation. They have identified the products, services, processes, business units, and markets that need improvement and those that need to be withdrawn from production lines. They are prepared ahead of time to relaunch as soon as they reach their inflection point. Proactively reacting to their market conditions gives them an undue advantage over their competitors. Leading companies have taken this to a whole new level by setting the trend in their industries, only to leave others to follow. This advantageous position enables them to rapidly gain market share while growing their revenues at a relatively lower cost.

The digitalised economy has been set aside by its unique characteristics, the key being personalisation led by innovation and disruption. Personalisation of products and services has led to higher expectations from individuals, which has led to hyper-personalisation and continuous disruptions to operating models. As a result of the continuous disruptions, the distances between the points of inflection have gotten shorter, which has led to a continuous series of improvements at each inflection point. For organisations paralysed by this dynamic shift in their ecosystem or drowned with continuous analyses and what-if scenarios or for those that have remained oblivious to these disruptive shifts, the path has been a one-way road to irrelevance or even extinction.

The impact of disruption varies across individuals and organisations. The key is to proactively recognise it and swiftly act to make incremental progress. With progressive steps, the dark tunnel ahead of them begins to emit its own light, enough to help them move to the next progressive step. As they gain confidence, they begin to comprehend that the basic principles of survival at each inflection point are to move fast, embrace change, adapt quickly, and think innovatively to win.

Exercise:

Take the below exercise to understand your points of inflection:

1. List down the points of inflection, when you had to change course to achieve your previous goals.
2. List down what you did to adapt to the new course.
3. List down what you could have done differently knowing what you now know.
4. List down your current position w.r.t your current goals.
5. Identify your next point of inflection to achieve your goals.

4.3 Power of Your Visualisation

All that we are is the result of
what we have thought.

—Buddha

In the past, when you wanted something bad and it meant a lot for you to get it, more often than not, you got it. When your goal was to buy a new car, you got it; if you wanted to buy a new house, you got it; if you wanted to take that exquisite vacation, you went on it; or if you wanted to get that new job, you got it.

Roll back and think about what happened during each of these times. Your strong desire to make this happen backed by your persistence ensured it happened. This was all driven by the image of your desired object that you formed and placed in your mind. The mind then worked its magic to make it happen and achieve your goals. When the mind is channelised with past successes, it generates positive inner energy.

A picture speaks a thousand words; we all know this is the most apt way to communicate a message to an audience in a fraction of a second. Our minds are complex processing units. It processes what we have planted in our minds in a subconscious way. While the mind is complex and powerful, it rarely erases an image or an incident that it has processed and subconsciously stores in the brain.

Imagine the power of the mind if it is made to visualise, a future achieved state every day. The image eventually gets engraved in the person's mind. Both the conscious and subconscious minds believe that the future state (the planted image) has been achieved, which then controls our actions to make sure we achieve that future state.

It is amazing to witness parents who planted into their children's minds a future picture of being a doctor, engineer, banker, scientist, musician, or athlete all through their childhood. These children grew up to be in the same profession of their future image. The amazing aspect is the path the child has taken, both consciously and subconsciously, in reaching their end state. The picture of the end state gets deeply rooted in the child's mind. The roots of the image grow deeper and deeper with each successful step. The image becomes clearer and opens the path to further progress. As adults, we do the same. Whatever our wish may be, we start our journey by forming a picture of it in our minds. The more we want it, the clearer is the picture in our minds. Once the picture is formed in our minds, we subconsciously work relentlessly towards achieving it.

What you see is what you get

People who wish to buy a house would have a mental picture of their dream house in their mind in terms of the location, community, the colour of the rooms, type of kitchen, bedroom, garage, views from each of the rooms, swimming pool, play area, gym, etc. As they internalise that wish in their mind, they would start looking out for the price, then work out the mortgage plans and arrive at how much they would need to save in order to make the down payment to secure the home loan. They would work out the monthly instalments. Their mind would shift from just wishing to doing. They would shift into an execution mode of making it happen, struggling at first but then overcoming all limitations to making it happen. They would save money to make the down payment and contact the bank to formalise their mortgage, and by the time they know it, they are well and truly on their journey to owning a house.

People who wish to change their jobs to a new location in a larger and better company would dream of relocating to a new work environment. They would think about the new city where the office is located, the brand recognition of the prospective employee, their products, esteemed customers, and everything else associated with them. They would review what the potential role would be along with its responsibilities. They would even get smarter by assessing their current skills against the potential jobs and subconsciously work on developing new skills to bridge the skill gap.

As individuals go through these steps, the mind develops a clear image and a strong conviction about making this image a reality. The more frequently the future image is viewed and reflected upon, the more it influences the person's actions to achieve it. The internal forces within the individual's system and all external forces gravitate together and work in harmony to help the individual reach that future image.

Communicate with visualisation

Visualisation has helped leaders communicate where their company is headed. More importantly, they paint a picture of what they want their leaders to achieve. Some companies use the concept of a vision board that helps their teams visualise their end state. Very often when a business sets its annual or five-year targets, they build a theme, an image, and a slogan that remind their employees of the larger picture that they need to achieve. Organisations have used the visualisation technique to launch new businesses, enter new markets, gain market shares, win deals, negotiate for win-win, and much more.

A few years ago, a regional company wanted to expand its geographic reach to the African market. It had a clear vision of expanding to specific industries and specific countries in the African continent. The CEO made it a point to spend a few minutes in his weekly leadership meetings to not only talk about the African market but to also promote it as a holiday destination for his team's next vacation. He handed over the map of Africa with the target countries highlighted and requested each of his leaders to pin this map in their offices.

In six months, the company had achieved its annual goal of expanding into the African continent. Their business grew both in revenues and profitability, with each of the leaders taking home a lucrative bonus package. Interestingly, the leadership team not only vacationed in some of these countries but also promoted the destinations to their larger families and friends. They gained the mindshare to expand to those countries and established common friends and business associates, who in turn helped them establish their presence faster than they had initially envisaged. By visualising an image of the company's expansion into the African market, the team developed a mindshare that was planted by their CEO.

Exercise:
To build your own your visualisation, follow the below steps:

1. Know the end state of what you want to achieve.
2. Identify an image/picture that communicates your end state in detail.
3. Pin up this picture where you can see it throughout the day.
4. Take a few seconds to visualise this image with your eyes closed.
5. Think of all the things you need to do that will bring you closer to this image.
6. Repeatedly tell yourself with full faith that you will achieve this end state.
7. Talk to your family and close friends to gain encouragement and to strengthen the commitment.

Building your vision board

Each year, I would create my vision board of things I needed to accomplish for that year. For instance, my vision board would have pictures of my family (normally placed in the centre), the house I plan to buy, the places I want to visit, specific areas to improve myself, certification and courses to be completed, and so on. At the start of the year, I would collect the pictures and pin them on a corkboard beside my study table; I did this every year to form an image of the goals I had to accomplish.

You could build your own vision board by adding pictures, words, quotes, or cutting them from magazines, newspapers, photographs, or even lightweight objects that could be pinned or glued to your vision board. While building your vision board, pick only those images, words, or quotes that truly resonate with your life goals and future state. Include your name with the date at the right or left bottom of the vision board. Your vision board could be a simple chart, cork sheet, or even a cardboard sheet.

Keep your vision board in a visible place that would allow you to see it frequently, just before going to bed and first thing when you wake up in the morning. Allow your mind to wander as you stare at your vision board. Some days you may draw a blank, or on some other days, you may draw deep inspiration from the vision board. Let your mind go with the flow of nature, and let your imagination run wild with no limitations. Let the thoughts of your future accomplished state sink into your mind, and it will allow Mother Nature to subtly trigger its law of attraction, as proclaimed by Napoleon Hill. The law of attraction will draw all people and resources necessary to achieve the images on your vision board.

The vision board subconsciously works on the mind and forms a future image in your mind. The mind is not able to interpret if the image is past, present, or future. By visually seeing the pictures, the mind assumes that your future state has been achieved. The subconscious mind and the conscious mind work together, and the vision board slowly but surely begins to become a reality.

As you accomplish your goals, stick a golden or silver star on top of the pictures on your vision board. These stars are to recognise and acknowledge the accomplishments of your goals. The law of attraction works in mysterious ways, bringing you closer with each accomplishment of your goal. The goals depicted on the vision board work like they are the centre of gravity, and everyone and everything conspires to work towards the fulfilment of that goal. This positive reinforcement produced by the law of attraction will motivate you further to complete your remaining goals. As you progress, you will experience an effortless journey towards the fulfilment of your goals.

Below is a classic example of a vision board from the legendary Oprah Winfrey.

Notice how she has positioned her own photograph at the centre of the vision board. By doing so, the personalised power that the vision board generates is tremendous. After all, the vision board is about achieving the goals you set for yourself.

You could also create a vision board for your business as below.

Whatever it is you want to truly achieve, it could be finding a spouse, getting a new job, relocating to a new country, or starting a new business, you can achieve this by first building your vision board.

Power of having a structure

When pursuing goals, besides visualising your end state, there is tremendous benefit in selecting and keeping a "structure." A structure is a physical object that will remind you of your life purpose, vision, goals, and objectives. It should instantaneously help you relate to your life purpose. If your end goal is to write a book, you could keep a small book on your study table; if your goal is to represent your school or college football team, then you could keep a football by your bedside; if your goal is to join your dream company, then you could keep that company's printed logo on your table. There are several ways in which you could build a structure. The key is to ensure that the structure you select resonates with you. It should instantly resonate with your life purpose and goals. You should feel an instant surge in energy or resonance when you see your structure.

Structures ensure that goals enter your conscious mind and feed into the subconscious mind. You reach a point when you may not even notice the structure in front of you. This is the time to replace it with a new structure or just add another structure along with it, as you may have developed some bonding with your earlier structure.

4.4 Build Your Mastermind by Gaining Mindshare

Some people have a natural tendency to attract followers; they have gained the mindshare of a core group of people. This core group of people, in turn, influence their inner circles, and it cascades further down the chain. They have successfully built common mindshare across the group with an intense focus on achieving a common goal. They are like an orchestra directed by a conductor with a common goal of playing their symphony to perfection. Higher the mindshare and orchestration, better the performance and music.

Parents have a natural instinct to ensure that their families always stay together, even in difficult times. Some may argue that this has not been the case with their parents. At times, the inherent natural instinct in parents may have not been used due to their circumstances. Parents decide on their family goals, which sometimes are their individual goals, for the benefit of the family. Their individual goals may include a better job, moving to a better or new location, buying a new house, and more, to provide a better life for their family.

Stan's parents decided that on completion of his high school he would graduate to be an engineer. He would also be an all-rounder, both in academics and at sports. They wanted Stan to become a role model for his friends and other children. This was a huge task, given that Stan was a mischievous child with poor concentration.

Stan's parents went about their task undeterred by his behaviour and performance at school. At the dinner table, they would talk about how Stan would graduate to be an engineer in a few years and the kind of life he would have for himself and his family. They added that on the way to becoming an engineer, he would do well both in his academics and in sports. They even went on to say that the school would realise Stan's unique hidden leadership qualities. And someday soon, the school would make Stan a school prefect and a house captain.

Stan's parents were using the power of visualisation by creating a dream (future image) about him. They painted the future picture of Stan being an engineer and then talked about how it would unfold for him, along the way. They knew he was a child with potential if he channelised his efforts and stayed focussed on his goals.

Stan's parents would take turns talking to him. They learned that as a child he was emotional and empathetic in almost all situations. He was a loving child who never disrespected them. While his IQ (intelligent quotient) was above average, his EQ (emotional quotient) was the highest they had seen in any child his age.

After several months, this got internalised within Stan's mind. His parents had slowly but surely gained his mindshare of what they wanted their son to achieve. Soon he started dreaming that one day he would become a prefect, a house captain, and an engineer. He would make his parents, family, and friends proud. More importantly, he would make himself proud.

Stan kept visualising the image his parents had planted in his mind. By creating this image in his mind, they, in fact, gained the mindshare of the goal they wanted their son to achieve. With each passing month, the image got bigger and clearer, until it took a central place in his mind. They had sown the seeds of a mastermind, and the entire family resonated to help Stan achieve his goals.

In a few years, Stan went to complete his primary school in the science stream. He went on to become a prefect in his eleventh grade, followed by being a house captain a year later. He dramatically improved in sports, winning several medals and trophies. Four years after completing high school, he successfully graduated in engineering.

When the mind visualises a future image, the body, mind, and soul work together to create a mastermind. The internal and external forces then align with this mastermind to achieve the future state. When the belief in one's goal is high with undeterred conviction, the universal forces will work in harmony to help them achieve it. This goal becomes the new centre of gravity until it is achieved.

Organisations must build their employees' mindshare about their goals and how they would go about achieving them. They should have a regular flow of communication backed by focussed meetings and workshops. They must break down the five-, three-, and one-year goals into quarterly goals like steps to climbing up the ladder. They must paint a picture of how the company will achieve these quarterly goals in the first year and how this sets the stage for achieving their three- and five-year goals. Employees look for conviction from their stakeholders in the goals set by the company. Higher the conviction, higher is the probability that all employees will gain the mindshare to build a mastermind and achieve the company's goals.

Organisations must reinforce the image of their long-term goals and display it at key points across locations within the company. It is like a brand building and promotion exercise. Slowly but surely, the image gets formed into people's minds. The mind blocks get replaced by the end state image. Employees' minds shift from why they cannot achieve to how they will achieve their goals. In the process, the organisation creates a mastermind of its goals.

Ironically, there would be a small percentage of the team that is not aligned to the mastermind of the company. Let us call them the *drifters*. Leaders should spend extra time and effort to onboard them into the company's mastermind, but within a defined period. A single dissonance within the team is enough to cause disruptions in the team's attention towards the prime goal. Should they still fail to onboard the *drifters*, then they should move on to the next best option, which is to release them from their team, unit, or even the company. These are the weeds that will prevent the company from building its mastermind and progressing.

The steps to creating a mastermind

1. Identify your life purpose or vision and mission.
2. List down the short-, mid-, and long-term goals.
3. Establish a core mastermind group of like-minded people.

4. Build mindshare across the ecosystem with a future image.
5. Force multiply and grow the mastermind through the core mastermind group.
6. Identify the drifters and work towards onboarding them.
7. Release or replace the drifters to establish a cohesive mastermind.

4.5 Align Your Body, Mind, and Soul (BMS)

The body, mind, and soul form the fundamental of your being and existence. At the core of your system is your soul. Your soul is the centrifugal force that resonates with your life purpose. The resonance and vibrations within you get so high that you instantaneously know when you have found your life purpose. It is like falling in love for the first time.

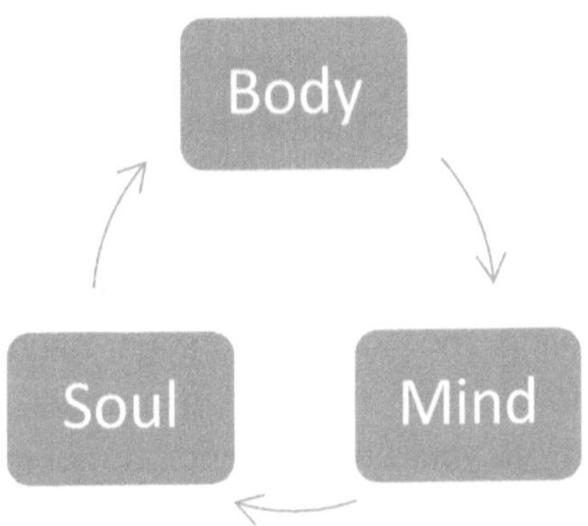

Your life purpose originates from your soul and subconsciously energises you to move forward in the right direction. Your soul ensures that the mind places your life purpose at the centre stage. The mind then energises the body to take the necessary action.

Your body builds a natural alliance and alignment with your life purpose and is largely driven by your conscious and subconscious minds. To achieve your life purpose, you need to build short-, mid-, and long-term goals that are in complete alignment with each other, and are in resonance with your life purpose.

The powerful alignment of your life purpose with your soul, mind, and body provides you with the universal force to relentlessly pursue your goals. All forces within you and around you work in harmony with each other to ensure the achievement of your goals, provided you stay the course with discipline and perseverance.

When your body, mind, and soul are aligned with each other, they are all in harmony with your life purpose. Your mind eliminates the blocks that prevent you from visualising your goals. With stronger visualisation of your goals, you gain inner mindshare towards the achievement of your goals. This inner mindshare radiates unprecedented levels of positive energy outward to gain mindshare from your ecosystem. In the process, you establish a mastermind of the goals you want to achieve. The universe is made up of living and non-living things, each with their own magnetic field force. The mastermind attracts both living and non-living things into your universe and harmoniously align them to help you achieve your goals.

Exercise:
Spend at least ten minutes early morning or at night being mindful of the body, mind, and soul alignment. Listen to the thoughts that enter into your mind and appreciate them. Do not judge them; just acknowledge their interim existence as they fade away.

4.6 Realign with Your Constraints

*Genius is one per cent inspiration, ninety-nine
per cent perspiration.*

—Thomas A. Edison

By now, you have understood how to build your mastermind by gaining mindshare and aligning your body, mind, and soul in total harmony. We move to the next step of knowing what constraints are, why do you need to manage them, and how to do that.

Constraints, in the simplest form, are the limitations holding you back from achieving your goals. Constraints take several forms; they could be in your minds, or they could be genuine limitations due to lack of knowledge and skills, or externally driven constraints over which you have little control. Knowing the type of constraints will enable you to manage them accordingly.

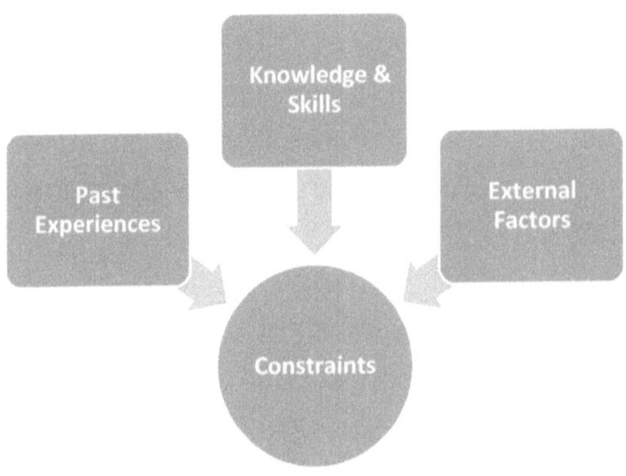

The first type is constraints that are in people's minds; they are driven largely by *unsuccessful past experiences*, also called as mental blocks. These past experiences have a stickiness effect and tend to leave a scar in the memory bank. The next time if a similar situation arises, our minds are preconfigured to think, "Oh boy! I have been through this before and don't believe it can be done, just like last time."

The second type is constraints driven from *lack of knowledge and skills.* You either have the knowledge and skills to undertake the tasks or you do not. If you are somewhere in between, then it is a question of how much time you need to acquire the necessary knowledge and skills. A degree of complexity comes into play here.

Higher the complexity, the longer will be the time required to acquire the necessary knowledge and skills. For instance, learning a new programming language to make yourself eligible for a prestigious project would require months of efforts. Likewise, lower the complexity, faster will be the time required to acquire the knowledge and skills. For instance, if you need to relocate to a new city, you intuitively know what needs to be done. You will research the place, discuss with family, friends, and colleagues, and join a local club online. In a few weeks, you would have jump-started your knowledge about the city to plan your relocation.

The third type is constraints driven by *external factors* that tend to be less in your control. This could be due to several factors such as political, economic, market, competition, customer, and financial. While you may not have control over these, you can proactively scan the environment for early warning signals to understand the impact on your position and existence. This would enable you to proactively take the precautionary measures ahead of time.

So why do you need to manage constraints?

If you have a vehicle breakdown, your journey does not end. You fix it or hitch a ride or rent another vehicle and continue your journey. Imagine for a moment what life would be if you had a "can-do attitude" to anything that came your way. You would progress in life, no matter what the odds are. Constraints are like barriers that slow you down from completing your journey. The better managed they are, the higher is your probability of overcoming them.

How do you manage constraints?

Managing your constraints will depend on the type of constraint you encounter. The three different types of constraints we covered earlier in this chapter are constraints driven by past experiences, lack of knowledge/skills, and by external factors.

For constraints that are driven by past experiences, take the initiative to *win small-win fast* and commit to it. Take the necessary steps to achieve your first small win; this will give you the confidence to achieve another win, thereby having a powerful snowball effect. Even if you fail, quickly relate to your earlier wins. The mind tends to attract past failures rather than past successes. For instance, if you want to give up a vice or a bad habit, chunk it down and reduce the intake and then move to replace that habit with another good habit.

For constraints driven from a lack of knowledge and skills, this requires grit and determination to build your profile. Understand your needs, create a knowledge and skill plan, and commit to it. List down what skills you need to onboard and, in order to do that, what knowledge you need to acquire by when and how. For instance, if you need to improve on your soft skills like presentation or communication or negotiation skills, then get yourself trained.

For constraints driven by external factors, proactively establish your safety baseline to counter any undue circumstances. Firmly place in your mind that you can control everything within you and are prepared to bounce back, no matter what. For instance, if you are working in a highly disruptive industry, the chances of your position being disrupted are high. You need to have an alternative plan ready, like cross-skilling for another role or industry, should you need to shift tracks at short notice.

Exercise:

1. Knowing your current position, identify your clearly stated goals.
2. Identify the roadblocks that are holding you back. These could be fear of failure, habit of procrastination, addiction, lack of self-belief, fear of the unknown, competition, market, etc.
3. Shortlist that one big constraint that is holding you back from achieving your stated goals. The constraint that is blocking your path to progress.
4. Categorise these constraints into internal and external types. You are likely to realise that over 70 per cent of your constraints are internal. Do not worry about it.

5. Depending on the type of constraint, write down the following:

- What you must do to overcome that constraint.
- How will you do this?
- By when will you do this?
- Who can support you?

4.7 Your Personal Development Plan (PDP)

Now that you have your life purpose and goals defined, understood your points of inflection, and know how to manage constraints, we move to the next step of building a Personal Development Plan (PDP). Your PDP is a snapshot that once completed will be a tool to help you navigate your life journey. It is a living document that must be nourished every week. The nourishment is the validations of the actions you need to take, as planned, to accomplish your goals.

At one of the training sessions, I attended several years ago, the speaker asked the audience if they had a PDP in place. Not surprisingly, less than 10 per cent of the audience raised their hands to confirm they had a PDP in place. Interestingly over 70 per cent of the audience had no PDP. The balance 20 per cent wanted to have a PDP but never had the time to build one! The speaker went on to explain that without a PDP, your life is on an unchartered course. It is only a matter of time before which you realise that having a PDP and working towards it gives you a competitive edge. Furthermore, when you have a PDP that is regularly monitored, updated, and measured to accomplish your goals, you get a higher sense of accomplishment.

This is the purpose of a PDP; it drives you towards achieving your life purpose. The successful ones plan their future while living in the present. They have a life purpose and a plan to achieve it.

The point we miss is viewing life from a total integrated perspective—the perspective of our body, mind, and soul—which is internal to us—along with the perspective of our goals like personal, family and friends, health, professional, and knowledge, among others. Our lives, like other universal systems, must have all parts operating in harmony and resonating with each other. The failure of one part leads to the failure of the whole system.

Your PDP must be viewed from all the possible angles impacting your life. It does not matter what the impact is now, but it is essential that you factor it into your plan. People in their thirties enjoy their lives and live for the moment until they reach the forties and have their "Oops" moment. Their Oops moment is when they realise that they have achieved little in their personal lives, have not saved for their children's education and their retirement, and are saddled with unpaid mortgages.

4.8 Tools to Align

Personal Development Plan (PDP)

The PDP aligns everything together and directs you on what must be done to progress and elevate yourself.

At the very least, the PDP should capture your core competencies, skills, and knowledge you possess and wish to acquire; people who can support you; resources required; and lastly the deterrents you need to overcome in order to achieve your knowledge development goals.

Answering questions to all the factors will equip you and constructively guide you. You will progress forward with a sense of purpose and fulfilment knowing you are on the right track, and knowing what you need to be aware of.

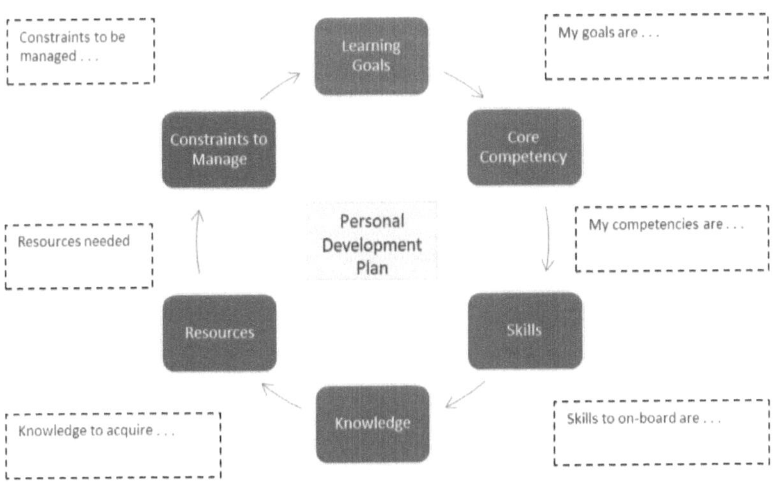

A simple template to help you get started that includes Area of Development, Category, Completion Date, How You Will achieve It (what needs to be done and who will help you), and Review Dates (weekly, fortnightly, or monthly).

My Personal Development Plan (PDP)					Date: xx-xx
My Goals:					
Areas of Development	PDP Category	End Date	What Is the Measure	How Will I Achieve It	Progress Review Date

GROW Model

Knowing your life purpose and what goals you must achieve is one thing. Setting your goals is another thing. **Sir John Whitmore**, famous for his **GROW Model** (Goal, Realistic, Option, and Way Forward) of coaching, came up with The **John Whitmore model** for setting goals.

The Whitmore model is made up of fourteen criteria to have the right goal. These criteria are segmented into three blocks across SMART, PURE, and CLEAR. SMART goals are Specific, Measurable, Attainable, Realistic, and Time Bound. PURE goals are Positively Stated, Understood, Relevant, and Ethical. CLEAR goals are Challenging, Legal, Environmentally Sound, Agreed, and Recorded.

The Whitmore model helps individuals with a clear focus on achieving the end goals while developing themselves. This could be applied to a team or to oneself. The model is purpose-driven and helps individuals align their goals with their life purpose, thereby ensuring that the process of goal attainment is an enjoyable one, backed by the individual's passion and, importantly, resonates with the individual's life purpose.

Chapter Five

Phase 3 — Transform

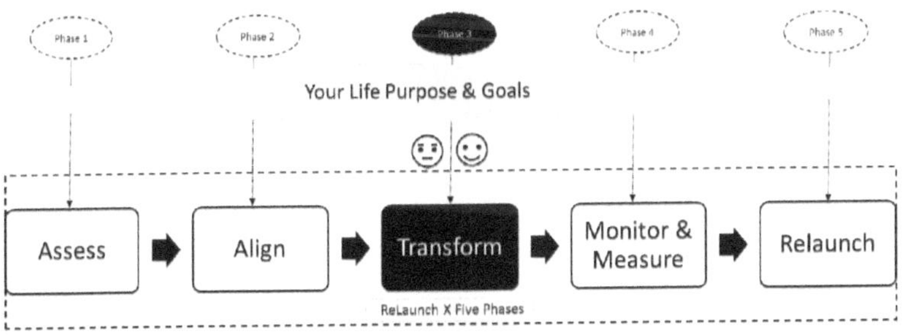

The best way to predict the future is to create it

—Peter F. Drucker

Congratulations! You have completed two phases of ReLaunch X. In the Assess phase, you identified where you are, where you want to be, and identified your life purpose. Next, in the Align phase, you identified your goals, how to manage your constraints, how to build a mastermind, and have a PDP. In the transformation phase, we will focus on the actions you need to take to bring about everlasting change and continuous improvement.

5.1 Align Transformation to Your Life Purpose

The best way to predict your future is to create it.

—Abraham Lincoln

There are several factors driving disruption in the new age digital world, and they are continuously changing the rules of the game. They are disrupting industries, markets, competition, companies, individuals, employment, the way we consume products, the way we buy, the way we sell, the way we communicate with each other, the way we work, the way we live, and the way we acquire skills and knowledge, among many other things. The new age world has made people's lives truly dynamic with the rapid pace of continuous changes. In this disarray of people's lives, it is imperative for people to have a defined life purpose that resonates with their body, mind, and soul. They should work on establishing the alignment between their life purpose and the transformation happening around them.

Leading companies are quickly losing their monopolistic position to the more agile start-up companies, which are faster to respond to market dynamics. This is no different for the organisation's workforce. Yesterday's highly skilled employees, who were unable to keep pace with the disruptive transformation happening around them, are losing opportunities to the younger new-skilled employees, and in the process threatening their very existence.

The skills and experience of yesterday's jobs may not be relevant to the new profiles of job positions being rapidly created and driven by complex customer demands, automation, and preferences of the new age economy.

Industries and organisations are forced to transform their business and operating models to keep pace with the market dynamics, driven by the new age digitalisation. This, in turn, mandates individuals to transform their work and personal lives. Individuals who have proactively prepared and have embarked on their transformation journey have an unfair advantage.

The driving factors for individuals to transform could be **Internal, External,** or **Situational**. Any change, whether Internal, External, or Situational, will first mandate a change from within. A change from within is prima facie an internal change. The more one adapts and proactively drives their internal transformation, the better prepared they will be to handle the external and situational factors. We cannot predict the external or situational factors and when they will happen, but what we can predict is how we can respond to them, based on the level of preparedness, driven by our internal transformation.

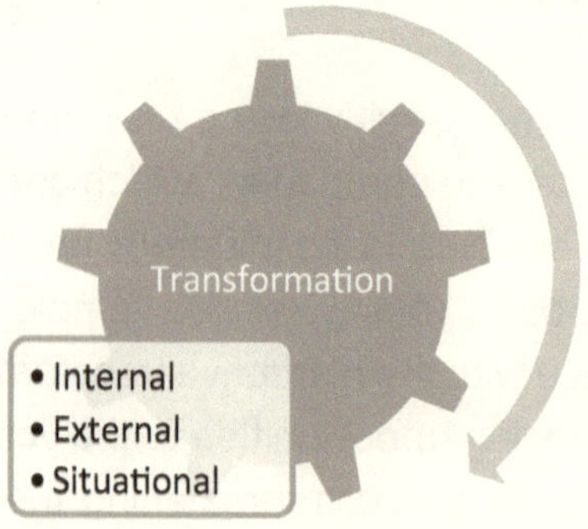

Internal transformation happens when you identify your life purpose and proactively work on a plan to transform yourself. Internal transformation is intrinsic and includes your short-, mid-, and long-term goals in mind. Focussing on internal transformation is key, as it allows you to remain in control, decide your path, and manage the outcomes. Internal transformation not only impacts external and situational transformations, but it also ensures that you will achieve your life purpose.

External transformation is when we witness or experience external changes approaching us and we are forced to proactively transform, else risk being made irrelevant or extinct. This transformation is driven by external forces acting or would act on us. It is like a storm approaching that we can intuitively sense heading our way.

Today's economy and markets are driven by digitalisation of business processes and tasks. This would, in effect, make some job roles extinct and force individuals to reskill themselves. For instance, the automobile industry is facing a similar situation with the launch of driverless cars. Auto manufacturers are now seeking innovative ways to manufacture driverless cars driven by new customer demands and new competitors. They understand that the earlier manufacturing processes will not hold good. They are forced to transform their products, accessories, suppliers, and manufacturing processes, which are now not only automated but also intelligently digitalised with a system that is developed using artificial intelligence and deep learning, leading to the advent of connected cars. The future connected car will understand their driver, predict their driving patterns as well as likes and dislikes concerning the routes they take, and take control when needed.

The impact on the automobile industry also has an effect on the auto insurance sector, with self-driven and intelligent, connected cars. The auto insurance sector may find that with more predictability in driving, there is a low probability of accidents on the road. This, in turn, would force them to lower their auto insurance premium. Insurance companies would be forced to transform and change their business and operating models or lay off and reduce their workforce. Like many other industries, the insurance industry is also going through its own forced transformation such as an automated renewal of insurance premiums driven by Robotic Process Automation.

Situational Transformation happens due to unplanned events. The situation could be pleasant or unpleasant. It could be as bad as having a car accident, being laid off, or losing a loved one, or as good as winning a lottery. Either situation would force you to react and instantly transform yourself on the spot.

For instance, your best performing team member has decided to quit, leaving you with the burden of finding a replacement while managing your job and filling the void created by his absence. It could be your spouse or partner who has been made redundant at work, leaving you to reorganise not only your finances but also your lifestyle. We also witness forced situational transformation when individuals transform themselves depending on the situation, like during the different stages of a negotiation process. It is amazing how experienced negotiators seamlessly transform themselves to adapt to the negotiation process.

Transformation starts and ends with transforming from within. The choice of a proactive or reactive transformation is in your hands.

When you keep your mind agile, alert, and aligned to your life purpose, it automatically remains alert, proactive, and adaptive to virtually any change that comes your way. When the body, mind, and soul is undergoing continuous internal transformation, it is prepared to make transformation a way of life.

5.2 Understand the Change Process . . . To Embrace It

Anybody can change, but they have
to want to change.

—Marshall Goldsmith

Categorising the forces driving transformation will help an individual understand the internal, external, and situational factors affecting their transformation. This would enable them to prepare accordingly. In this section, we will outline the transformation cycle and how understanding this cycle helps individuals to progress through their own change cycle.

Let us take a step back and look at how organisations manage, change, and apply those learnings to how individuals can manage their own change. Organisation Change Management is simpler to plan yet complex to execute and experience. There are several factors that come into play. On the one hand, we have factors such as the organisation's vision, mission, values, new goals, and business plans, and more. On the other hand, we have factors such as an individual's aspirations, values, goals, skills, competencies, and more. The challenge is in getting the two categories to resonate in harmony with each other.

Change management models

Today, organisations have successfully adopted several change management models to drive transformation. Some of the commonly adopted organisation change management models include *The McKinsey 7S Model, Lewin's Change Management Model, Kotter's Change Management Model, Bridges' Transition Model, Roger Tech Adoption Curve,* and other models. Organisations have used the below change management models with a focus on their employees. The Individual Change Management models include *Kübler-Ross' Change Curve, Prosci ADKAR Model, and Nudge theory; Virginia Satir's family reconstruction therapy; Switch Way,* among others.

The objective of this book and section is not to dwell into these change management models but rather to understand how the change process works relevant from an individual's perspective. There are several books and articles from the original authors that provide a detailed and in-depth view of these change management models. Understanding these models and applying them to an individual's change management journey will allow individuals to embrace change more willingly and in the process, transform themselves and their ecosystem.

When individuals undergo any kind of transformation, their perspectives, confidence, behaviours, and reactions are shaped by the different emotions they experience at various stages of the change process. The Kübler-Ross' Change Curve is a model to adopt while addressing **Individual Change Management**. This in no way lowers the significance of the other change management models. The selection of which change management model to adopt is ultimately the choice made by organisations and individuals.

Kübler-Ross model for individual change management

The **Kübler-Ross Model** focusses on capturing the emotions of the individual at different phases of the Change Curve and can be applied by both organisations and individuals. The model has five stages starting with *Denial, Frustration, Depression, Experiment,* and *Decision.* In each of these stages, an individual experiences varying emotions driven by the internal, external, and situational factors of the transformation. *This model was developed by Elisabeth Kübler-Ross.*

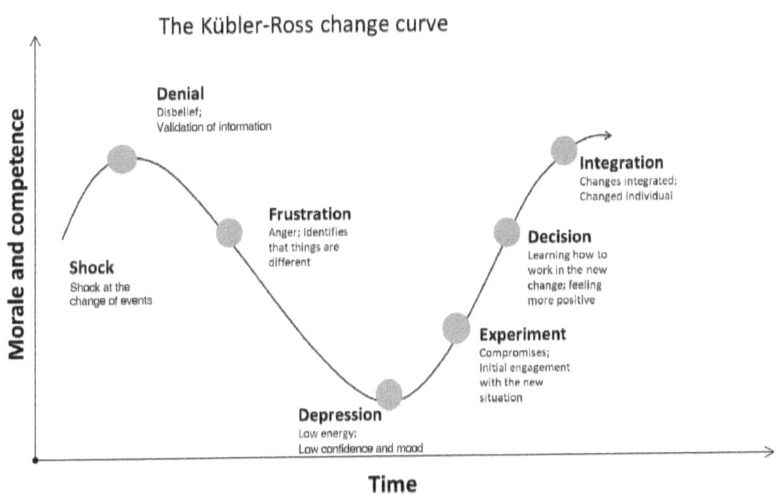

The Kübler-Ross model is a five-stage model.

Denial—This is the first stage when an individual is unable to accept the news and development. It is a smokescreen that a person tends to fictitiously create due to their inability to comprehend and accept the news. The individual experiences disbelief, looking for evidence that the news is not true.

Anger—When the news gets internalised within them, the individual's first reaction is anger and frustration as they realise the change is for real and it will impact them. They begin to react and demonstrate their anger.

Bargaining—Anger is followed by bargaining, when individuals bargain to get the best possible solution out of their situation. Bargaining is also a way for people to avoid losing face or ending up with a raw deal.

Depression—When the individual realises that his/her bargaining or negotiations will not work, they end up getting depressed and tend to lose hope. In this phase, the individual is oblivious to his surroundings, and his mind slips into a state of helplessness. In other words, the individual shifts into depression and this can be identified by their behaviours, mood swings, lack of commitment, and low energy and enthusiasm levels.

Acceptance—In this stage, realisation sets in for these individuals, and they come to terms with themselves. They realise that the new paradigm is here to stay, and they stop fighting against it and accept the change and the developments around it. Individuals explore all the options available to them to leverage their position. They learn how to work with the new situation.

Example of individual change management at work
Take the example of an individual who was expecting a promotion at work. She gets the surprising news that she is transferred to another department, in a different role. This was a result of the organisation's decision to change the existing

company structure and associated roles, as per their new business plans. The individual's initial reaction will be of being *shocked* as she was expecting a promotion but is instead being laterally moved. This would follow with a *denial* of what just happened.

She thinks there must have been a mistake. She goes through *frustrations* as her mind is in dissonance with the reality of what just happened. She then tries to *bargain* and pushes hard to win a promotion either in the same department or another department. She soon realises that this new change will not accommodate her aspirations. *Depression* follows, leading to low energy levels, self-pity, and low self-esteem for not being recognised with a promotion. She fails to see the organisation's bigger picture of driving these new changes.

After a few weeks, she begins to *experiment* with various thoughts about her new role in the new department. She consults with colleagues from different departments to get their perspectives. She tries to understand the benefits of the new role to her and the organisation. She realises that the reorganisation was driven by disruptive market dynamics and the organisation had to respond swiftly.

She, being a high performer, was reallocated to another business unit, since her previous unit would now get merged with the new business unit. She also realises that her skills are not fully up-to-date and she needs to quickly acquire the new skills and knowledge. She feels this change will help her improve and enhance her career.

She decides to have an open mind and begins to embrace her new role with newfound energy. She learns about the new role, understands the job description, and does a fit-gap analysis of her skills versus the new job role requirements. She builds a personal development plan on how she will engage in this new role, what new knowledge and skills are needed, identifies the people who can help her, and allocates time to complete her onboarding into the new role. In the process, she *integrates* into the reorganisation by first transforming herself.

Conscious Competence learning model

Another commonly adopted model is the **Conscious Competence learning model** which explains the different stages of learning a new skill or behaviour. This model plots performance on the Y-axis with time on the X-axis. There are four steps to this learning model.

Management trainer Martin M. Broadwell described the model as "the four levels of teaching" in February 1969.

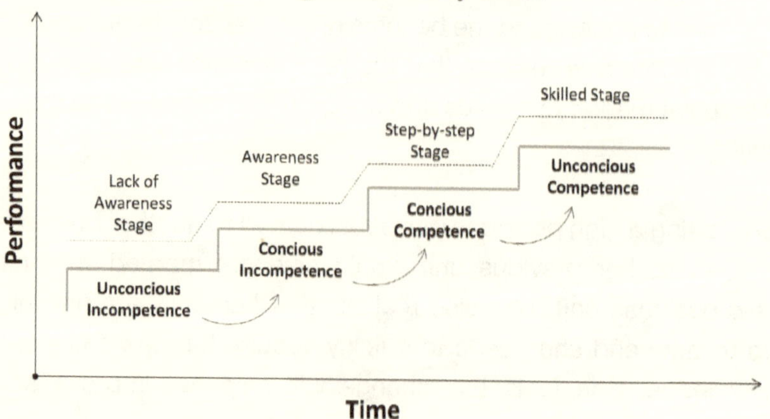

Step 1—unconscious incompetence
In this step, the individual is not aware of the existence or relevance of the skill area. They have a deficiency in the defined area. They might deny the relevance or usefulness of the new skill. The individual must become conscious of their incompetence before the development of the new skill.

Step 2—conscious incompetence
The individual becomes aware of the existence and relevance of the skill and is also aware of their deficiency in this new area. They realise that by improving their skills and abilities, their productivity will improve. The individual commits to learn and practice the new skill to move to the conscious competence stage.

Step 3—conscious competence
The individual achieves conscious competence in a skill when they can perform it reliably at will without assistance.

Step 4—unconscious competence
The skill becomes so practiced that it enters the unconscious parts of the brain; it becomes second nature, like driving, cycling, swimming, etc.

Example of Conscious Competence learning model
Take the example of a technical person taking on a sales role in a different industry, a different company with completely different products, and in a new location. He is new to the products he is selling, new to the industry, and new to the company and the country, besides the new job role.

He is completely new to the ecosystem and must unlearn and relearn the intricacies of the new job. In the initial phase, he may not be conscious of his incompetency in selling the new product to new customers in a new industry and new market. In this stage, his sales and productivity levels are low as he is still early in his learning cycle. He is conscious of his limitations and begins to recognise his incompetency.

He realises that to progress he must quickly acquire new knowledge and skills while building new professional contacts, by attending local conferences and events. He builds his competency by learning, training, and practicing, thereby improving his productivity and leading to higher sales. He leverages his technical competency to build instant trust and relationships with his customers. He is now conscious of his new competency.

As he sells more and succeeds, selling the new products to new customers in a new market becomes his second nature. He moves to being unconscious about his competency. He progresses in his new role with ease and begins to support his colleagues to sell. In a matter of time, he becomes a top performer in the new role.

The powerful duo for individual change management
To arrive at a **powerful** combination, we now merge the two models (Kübler-Ross and Conscious-Competence learning models) and plot the four learning stages (Conscious-Competence learning model) on the Change Curve (Kübler-Ross' model). Refer to the below chart. We get the unique depiction of what happens to

individuals when they undergo a transformation process. The individual experiences various emotions when they are conscious of their incompetence. These are plotted as dotted lines in the chart below. These emotions gradually ease up as they embrace the new status quo and progress towards being competent.

In the Unconscious-Incompetence phase, they experience denial and fear of change. In the Conscious-Incompetence phase, they experience anger and resistance to accept the change. In the Conscious-Competence phase, they begin to start accepting the change. In the Unconscious-Competence phase, they start to experiment with the new status quo and eventually integrate with it.

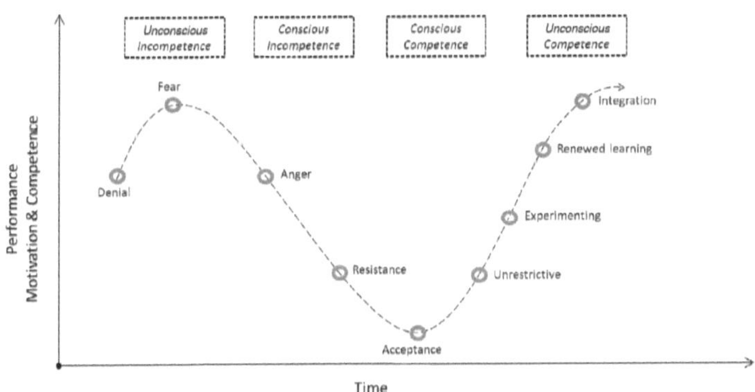

Capturing employees' emotions takes the experience journey to a whole new level. Organisations are in a better position to capture and understand the employees' experiences at different stages of their life cycle, including the change curve. Based on the feedback captured, organisations can up their game to improve the employees' experience, more so during a change.

Exercise

Spend the next few minutes to capture your experiences.

1. Write down the last time you underwent a change. This could be a relocation, promotion, new job, new role, or anything else that comes to your mind.
2. Reflect and write down your thoughts. Capture your thoughts and feelings before you start, the first few days, and later when you acquired the skills.
3. Map these on to the Individual Change Management model above

5.3 Overhaul Your Habits . . . Replace Old with New

Habits are deep-rooted behaviours we adopt over time. They are conscious and subconscious in nature. Habits could originate from our DNA or could originate from our influences acquired from our upbringing, namely our homes, family, friends, school, university, places of worship, social institutes, and our experiences in life.

We form opinions and values around our habits, thereby making it hard to let go. Habits get attached to people's values and attitudes. These can be constructive or destructive in nature. Take the case of a family who earns less but has the deep-rooted habit of saving the money they earn and investing their savings, compared to another family that earns twice as much, yet spends all their earnings and more.

The difference lies in the value system these families attach to the money they earned, saved, and invested. The first family honours the money they earn and respects it enough to save and invest it to build their future. Their value for money drives them to develop a constructive habit of saving and investing. Whereas the second family with different values has no consideration for their money;

they end up spending all their earnings, living a great life today, but leaving them with nothing for tomorrow. Their value for money has relegated them to develop a destructive habit of spending more than they earn.

As you embark on your transformation journey, you need to identify which one habit impacts 80 per cent of your life. You need to identify this one habit that holds you back from pursuing your dreams and life purpose. It could be procrastination, an addiction, overeating, too much time wasted on social media chats, wasteful browsing, or any other. It could also be allowing negative thoughts to percolate your mind from the time you wake up and leading you to not believe in yourself, thereby lowering your self-morale; or not letting go of past bad experiences and burning out your energy levels.

Exercise:

1. Identify one habit that has the greatest negative impact on your life. Write it down at the bottom of the paper, with black ink.
2. Take a moment to reflect on how your life would be if this habit did not exist in your life. Think of the things you could do when this one habit that has been holding you back is missing. Let your imagination flow, and do not be surprised if you get a sense of relief, knowing how constructive life would be without this one habit.
3. Now strike off the bad habit you wrote at the bottom of the paper, in red ink. Think of the one habit, which if immediately adopted by you, would propel you closer and faster to achieving your goals and life purpose.

4. Write this new habit down at the top of the same paper, above the old habit, in blue ink. Place this paper where you can see it daily. In this exercise, black ink denotes bad, red ink denotes to stop, and blue ink denotes a fresh start.

5. For the next thirty days, maintain an activity log of all the things you do from the time you wake up until the time you fall asleep. Look out for anything that would trigger your old habit against your specific activities and what time of the day it gets triggered. Reflect why it triggers you and what you wanted out of this activity. Be aware of when your trigger happens, against which specific activity, and why it triggers you. This is half the battle won. You then need to consciously control these triggers, before it controls you, for the first few weeks or months, until the old habit is quashed out.

Every habit has a place in your life. By removing an existing habit, it creates a void in your life. If this void is not quickly filled, either the old habit will slide its way back or another bad habit would take over the its place. To avoid this situation, you need to replace the old habit with your desired new habit.

Building new habits

A new habit starts with a desire to imbibe it. The desire for this new habit should be deep-rooted and aligned with your values. These are the sowing seeds to develop any new habit. If your desire to acquire new knowledge and skills is very high and is driven by a passion to bring out a shift in your life, then no matter what, you will invest time in reading and training yourself to acquire the new knowledge and skills. You will create space in your daily routine and steal an hour from your day to make this happen. If your life purpose is to touch people's lives by writing a book, then you will develop the habit of not only reading but also writing every day. This will enable you to publish your book.

A new habit, in general, takes at least three to six weeks to grow within you. But to drop an old habit, it takes months. It is only when you have committed in your mind to drop the old habit and that is backed by a strong desire to replace it with another new habit, will you be successful in bringing about this change. Your desire to embrace the new habit must be higher than your desire to hold on to the old habit.

Habits occupy a unique place in our daily lives and routines, making them difficult to drop, especially destructive ones. You need to replace the destructive habit from your systems with a constructive one. Your systems need to be taught to adopt a new habit, without leaving a void in your routines. Adopting the right habits forms the nucleus of your transformation.

The next time you spend time reflecting on yourself, think about how you gave up an old habit; think about how you acquired a new habit. You will be amazed how fast you acquired a new habit, whereas the old habit took time to let go. It took efforts to let go of an old habit, and it required discipline to stick with your decision to pursue your new habit. The energy required to build a new habit is effortless, whereas the effort required to drop a bad habit is a herculean task.

One evening, Henry was socialising with his friends at home. One of the men asked Henry how he had stopped smoking. He said it was a long story and maybe he will talk about it some other day. But they persuaded him to share his experience.

He said, "Oh well, OK, let me tell you the whole story. I attempted to stop smoking several times." His friends probed, "How many times?" He put his head down and said, "six times." This immediately brought a smile of acknowledgement among his friends. They had been through this many times and were keen to know how Henry had stopped smoking for the last eleven years!

He explained that he picked up the smoking habit from his college days. It became a social norm to smoke after every meal and get into general discussions. It was a great way to network and meet other students. This habit continued to his work and family life. He was keen to give up smoking, and several attempts to stop smoking in the past went in vain.

He analysed what made him quit smoking the last few times and what triggered him to start smoking again. Guilt and being health conscious helped him to stop smoking. He realised his trigger to start smoking was meeting up with old buddies, where he would have a few drinks, and that instigated him to have a couple of cigarettes as it was reminiscent of his past life. The following day he would have a huge sense of remorse. This disappointment worked against him, and he would start smoking again. He would give in to the "social peer pressure" and start smoking. His attempts to quit smoking would last a couple of months, and he would start overnight, triggered by a social get-together.

He decided that this time he would finally quit smoking. Over the years that followed, he met his buddies several times. After the first two meetings, they began supporting him and encouraging him to stop smoking. Over the course of time, one by one, all his buddies quit smoking, except for two. He also realised that he needed to change his routine at work. Instead of a smoking break, he shifted to having more frequent coffee breaks and catching up with colleagues over coffee.

As Henry was sharing his story on how he quit smoking, one of his friends asked why he loved chewing gum. He smiled and said that was his secret to dropping the smoking habit. He said, "You replace an old habit with another new habit. When I quit smoking, I realised that I needed to do something to replace my smoking habit. So, I figured that chewing gum or having an espresso shot made me feel good. Over time chewing gum and espresso replaced my habit of smoking."

He concluded with words of wisdom: Find a habit that you are passionate about. Eliminate the destructive habit to make the necessary space in your life. Replace the old habit with your new habit. To drop a habit, it must be replaced with another habit. The key is to find out what triggers the old habit, when does it trigger you, and why does it trigger you. You must change your daily routine without fighting the old habit.

5.4 Leverage Your Strengths . . . To Progress

Live as if you were to die tomorrow. Learn as if you were to live forever.

—Mahatma Gandhi

In a transformation journey, every individual must leverage their strengths while being mindful of their weaknesses. In the Assess phase, you listed down your strengths. Knowing your strengths will enable you to embark on your transformation journey, while managing your limitations.

The DNA of humans differs from individual to individual, and no two human DNAs are the same. Humans have natural strengths and weaknesses. There is no individual or organisation that exists without strengths. The difference lies in individuals who have identified their strengths and have leveraged them to perfection.

List your strengths and rank them in order of priority. Give yourself time to reflect when these strengths best resonated with you. This is to remind yourself and paint a picture of how you leveraged your strengths in the past. Identify what limitations you had in your personal and work life. Brainstorm how you plan to minimise the impact of your weaknesses. This could be acquiring new knowledge and skills, making new friends, onboarding new habits, and more.

Make a commitment to yourself, starting now, to leverage your top strengths. What action are you willing to take now that would leverage your strength and by when? What action are you willing to take now that would nullify your limitations and by when? Commit yourself to act on them!

Transformations have been successful when individuals have leveraged their strengths in full alignment with their life purpose and goals. The change they have undergone has been internalised and supported by their values. Core values influence the natural strengths, and secondary values influence the acquired strengths of an individual.

Relationship between your core values and natural strengths
Your core values are the source of your natural strengths. If your core value is to care for people, then your natural strength would be empathy. Your strength could be that you are empathetic to your customers, suppliers, and colleagues, thereby quick in establishing trust and building deep relationships. If your core value is perseverance, then your natural strength would be a commitment to outcomes or being result-oriented. This core value would make you highly committed to your job with a laser focus on achieving the desired results.

Your core values play a pivotal role in defining your natural strengths. When your natural strengths are not purposefully used in your daily life, they tend to fade away, yet always remain potent within you. On the other hand, when your natural strengths are used regularly in your daily activities, they tend to clearly define your character with a passion. This definition of your character is seamlessly in harmony with your life purpose and goals.

You need to reflect and understand what your core values are. Are your core values being used in your daily life? If not, how can you leverage your core values in your daily life? This will allow you to play on your strengths to progress ahead in your transformation journey.

A young individual with a natural flair for sales, working in a warehouse taking stock, may find his energy levels low at work. Over time, his natural strengths as a salesperson get dormant, yet he would still remain a natural salesman. He would consciously go about his job but with little or no happiness in the job. But when the same person is transferred to a sales role, his passion and natural strengths for sales make him a potential high performer. He performs the job with ease and more effectively compared to his earlier role.

Relationship between your secondary values and acquired strengths

Secondary values are the values that individuals onboard and gain during their lifetime. This is determined by the environment they are brought up in. This could be school, university, society, place of worship, workplace, friends, experiences they gained, and others. Their environment influences their acquired strengths. Let us say an individual's experience has been to establish rapport when meeting people for the first time. As a result of which he had great success in having a large network of friends. This experience would form his secondary value of being friendly and an extrovert. His acquired strength would make him a natural networker or connector who is comfortable meeting new people, making new friends, and being a social networker.

Having listed, ranked, and rated your strengths, you must now validate them for alignment with your life purpose and goals. You need to feel harmonised with your strengths as much as you feel harmonised with your life purpose. Applying your strengths to achieving your goals is key in your transformation journey. The higher the harmonisation between your strengths and life purpose, the more seamless will be your transformation journey. Knowing your strengths will allow you to scale to your full potential.

Focus 80 per cent of your time on leveraging your strengths and 20 per cent of your time on managing your limitations. Your strengths are the engine that will drive you to where you want to be. That said, one should not totally ignore the weaknesses. Acknowledging and being aware of them is crucial for your continuous improvement. Weaknesses are like roadblocks. They are here to stay, and maneuvering them is key to overcoming them.

5.5 Commit to Continuous Learning . . . Differentiate with Knowledge and Skills

Once you stop learning, you start dying.

—Albert Einstein

The last decade has witnessed tremendous change and disruption. The next decade will continue to witness more disruption, leading to unprecedented change. The key to remaining relevant is the unquenching thirst to continually acquire new knowledge, skills, and competencies.

As you embark on your transformation journey, you must continuously assess the relevance of your current knowledge and skills to achieve your stated goal. Ask yourself the question: "Knowing my life purpose and competencies, do I have all the necessary knowledge and skills to reach my destination?" This question would trigger the brain to identify the gaps needed to bridge the required level of knowledge and skills.

The new digital age has brought about disruption not only in new knowledge and skills but also in the way it is acquired and consumed. Individuals who regularly update their knowledge and skills are in constant demand for new roles and positions. They become the natural choice to take on new roles and remain in a superior position.

Acquiring new knowledge and skills has additional benefits to an individual. It helps develop expertise with a broader horizon, which in turn helps in having engaging conversations with various people. Importantly, it helps one develop higher self-esteem and self-confidence, and strengthens their pursuit to acquire more knowledge and skills. Commit to start now by identifying the areas you want to learn, and how you will achieve and leverage this newfound knowledge.

Learning is a continuous and consistent process, not a surge activity. It requires an individual to continuously assess what new knowledge and skills need to be acquired. Forward thinking organisations have quarterly essential learnings. These essential learnings or trainings are tailored for the individual's role. Furthermore, each employee, as part of their key performance indicators, is tasked with completing this essential learning within that quarter.

Exercise:
The following steps would help in building your knowledge and skills repository.

1. Identify the core areas of your work and personal life.
2. List down your goals that are aligned to your life purpose.
3. Against each goal, write down the knowledge and skills required to achieve that goal.

4. Rate your current knowledge and skill levels required to achieve your goals. This will give you a clear indication of how well positioned you are to achieve your goals.

5. Identify your knowledge and skill gap. The gap outlines what new knowledge and skills you need to acquire to help you achieve your goals. If you desire to seek a job into sales, the gap identified could be presentation or negotiation skills. If you desire to be a manager, the gap identified could be delegation, problem-solving, or decision-making.

6. Based on the gap identified, develop a learning plan. This would include a list of all the knowledge and skills needed to bridge the gap. You could develop a weekly, monthly, and yearly learning plans.

7. Identify your learning style. It could be reading, listening, or viewing.

8. Identify the sources to develop your knowledge and skills. These could include online information, books, certification programs at work, personal development certification programs, short-term skill development courses (Finance for beginners, Networking, Communication, etc.).

9. Having bridged the gap, the key to remaining ahead is to adopt a culture of continuous learning—a *kaizen*-like culture of continuous improvement. Knowing where you want to be and the skills required, you should commit yourself to a continuous learning plan. The key is to dedicate at least one hour daily towards reading something new in your area of interest. That would add up to seven hours a week or twenty-eight hours a month of learning. You will

be amazed with the new knowledge you acquire at the end of the month.

10. Make it a point to share these learnings. Sharing knowledge will reinforce your understanding and make you a subject matter expert.

5.6 Manage Your Energy Levels . . . For High Productivity and Results

Everything is energy and that's all there is to it.
Match the frequency of the reality you want, and
you cannot help but get that reality. It can be no
other way. This is not philosophy. This is physics.

—Albert Einstein

Have you felt highly energised at certain times of the day and less energised at other times of the day? We all have different energy patterns that vary during the day and even during the different days of the week. There are certain hours of the day when your energy levels are the highest, probably the first hours in the morning or the late hours of the night. There are certain other hours of the day when your energy levels are the lowest, possibly the hour just after lunch, when the blood from the brain and body moves to digest the food in the stomach. There are certain days of the week when we feel low, possibly the first or last working day of the week. There are days when our energy levels are at the highest, possibly the second, third, and fourth days of the week.

Your energy levels impact your productivity levels and the tasks to be completed. So how do you manage your productivity levels when your energy levels vary? The answer to this is when your energy levels are high, you assign certain types of tasks; and when your energy levels are low, you assign certain other types of tasks. This way you ensure that the tasks you have assigned to yourself are completely aligned with your energy levels. The assignment of your task type will depend on its complexity and priority. High-priority and high-complexity tasks must be assigned when your energy levels are high.

The below exercise will help you to understand and assign tasks based on your priority, complexity, and energy levels.

Exercise:

1. List your tasks to be completed.
2. Categorise them into High Priority and Low Priority. Further, categorise the High-Priority tasks into Complex and Simple Tasks and the Low-Priority tasks into Complex and Simple Tasks.

Priority-Complexity Grid

Priority/Complexity	Simple Tasks	Complex Task
High Priority		
Low Priority		

3. Create your five energy zones as below or in any five to six time zones as per your choice:

Energy Zone	Time Zone	My Key Tasks
Energy Zone 1	5:00 a.m. to 9:00 a.m.	
Energy Zone 2	9:00 a.m. to 1:00 p.m.	
Energy Zone 3	1:00 p.m. to 3:00 p.m.	
Energy Zone 4	3:00 p.m. to 7:00 p.m.	
Energy Zone 5	7:00 p.m. to 10:00 p.m.	

The five energy zones have a cumulative total of seventeen hours, in a day to complete your tasks, both personal and professional. This leaves you with seven hours to sleep.

4. Identify your high-and low-energy zones. For most people, Zone 3 tends to be low energy as it is the hours after their meal. If you are an early bird, then probably Zones 1 and 2 are your high-energy zones. For nocturnal people, Zone 5 tends to be the high-energy zone.

5. Map the high-priority-complex tasks into your high-energy zones and your high-priority-simple tasks into your low-energy zones. This will ensure you have completed all your high-priority tasks for the day. You could undertake the low-priority tasks with whatever time is available during the day.

Mapping the complexity of tasks to energy levels will allow you to complete high-priority tasks more effectively. Imagine a day when high-priority tasks get completed on time and in the most effective manner. The key to this is in knowing your energy levels and mapping the tasks across the day into high- and low-energy zones.

Some high-priority-low-complexity tasks could include calling your child's schoolteacher, greeting your customers during the festival season or for their birthday, sending your customers a thank-you mail, or calling your parents to wish them on their anniversary.

Some high-priority-high-complexity tasks could include preparing a techno-commercial proposal for your client, responding to a customer escalation mail or call, resolving a dispute with a colleague or between your team members, preparing for an interview, preparing a business plan document, and closing a deal to meet your year-end targets.

For a great perspective on managing your energy, read *Manage Your Energy, Not Your Time* by Tony Schwartz and Catherine McCarthy.

Understanding your inner energy centres

The entire galaxy and universe are made up of supreme energy. Every living being in this universe possesses their own energy force within them, and human beings are no exception.

This energy force inside your body is spinning on a spindle. This spinning energy has seven centres in your body, starting at the base of your spine and then moving all the way up to the top of your head. These energy levels are called *Chakras* in Sanskrit, meaning Wheel. You could picture the seven energy centres are seven energy wheels in your body.

In a healthy, happy, balanced person, the seven chakras disseminate balanced amount of energy to the different parts of your body, mind, and soul. If one of your chakras is spinning too quickly or slowly, you would immediately know, provided you are mindful to the imbalances as and when they occur within you.

Understanding the seven chakras will make you aware of the natural energy cycles within your body and how to resonate with each chakra. This in turn, will help you connect your physical, emotional, and spiritual imbalances with the chakras that empower them. If any of these chakras get blocked, then you need to pay attention to it and bring back the energy balance. Balancing your chakras will allow you to lead a harmonious healthy life and in fulfilment with your life purpose.

The Seven Chakras or Energy Centres of Your Body	
1. Root chakra, which is at the base of the spine. 2. Sacral chakra, which is located just below the navel. 3. Solar Plexus chakra, which is located in the stomach area. 4. Heart chakra located at the centre of the chest. 5. Throat chakra located at the base of the throat. 6. Third Eye chakra located at the forehead, between the eyes. 7. Crown chakra located at the top of the head.	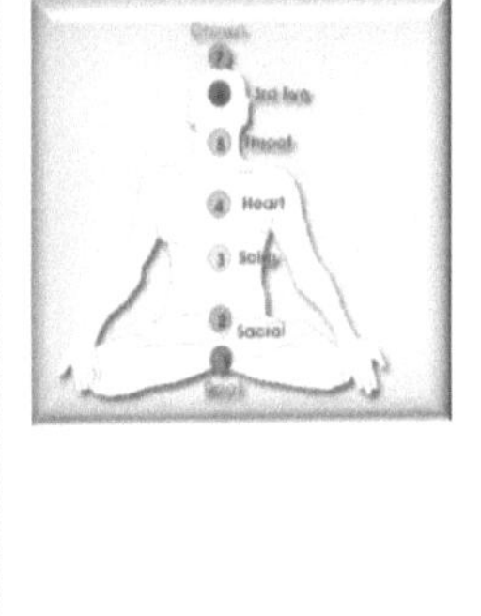

Managing your seven inner energy levels will allow you to have a balanced life. Managing your chakras would depend on the type of chakras. Broadly, chakras can be managed by regular meditation, being more mindful of yourself, balanced diet, routine yoga or physical activity, and having a positive outlook to everything that life has given you. Understanding chakras and managing them is an ancient technique by itself and is worth exploring in more detail.

Take time to reflect on your day's activities and achievements and visualise how your next day would look like and what would you like to change and prioritise. During the day, be mindful of where you are and whom you interact with; the activities you undertake should be in resonance with your life purpose. Do not be harsh in judging yourself; only focus on the progressive path you need to take to complete your tasks.

5.7 Manage Your Time . . . Have a Daily Ritual

Transformation is a journey where the only constant is Time. No matter which part of the relaunch cycle you are in now, there is a list of tasks and activities you must complete to propel further into the orbit. Having your life purpose and goals firmly placed in your mind  like the North star, the key is to assess and identify what tasks must be accomplished to take you closer to your goals. The urgency of some tasks will be relatively higher depending on the criticality of your current situation.

There is a cost associated with not completing your tasks on time or altogether neglecting them. The more critical and important a task is, the higher is the cost associated with it. We refer to cost not just in dollar terms but also in terms of impact, opportunity loss, and quality of life. As undone tasks move into a critical stage (important/urgent quadrant), the urgency of getting them is high and the impact of not getting them done is higher.

One wonders why people plan and yet fail to achieve their stated plan. While there could be several reasons for a failed plan, one of the primary reasons is the inability to complete or execute the planned tasks on time. The question that surfaces to mind is how can they plan their activities to help achieve their daily, weekly, monthly, and annual goals. The key to this is time management and how you manage your time to achieve more, both at work and at home.

People have thrived on building high-level plans with definite goals and then pursuing them with single-minded determination. They realised that some detailed planning, especially when you have limited time and resources, helps your cause in completing your tasks on time and achieving your goals. The key to managing your time is planning and execution. Having planned and set goals for yourself, the key to achieving these goals is execution within the stipulated time frame. Managing your time will enable you to optimally manage your resources and thereby predictably manage the outcomes. Effective time management of your tasks will also enable you to mitigate risks and proactively build in contingency plans. This will ensure that no matter what happens, you will meet your end objectives.

Exercise:
Below are the steps to help you mange time effectively:

1. Write down your long-, mid-, and short-term goals in three rows.
2. On a separate sheet of paper, write down every activity that comes to your mind that you must do in order to meet your goals.
3. Once you have completed your listing of pending activities, organise these tasks/activities by Long (L), Mid (M), and Short (S) term goals.
4. You can segregate your tasks as follows:
   - Tasks that are important and urgent must be addressed now, else they could jeopardise your position.

- Tasks that are important and not urgent must be addressed with a strategic mindset. These are the tasks if not addressed well ahead of time would soon become critical.
- Tasks that are not important can wait or be dropped.
5. Write down the date when you plan to complete each of these tasks.
6. Next is to prioritise your tasks into P1, P2, P3.

Urgent/Important Grid with Priorities

	Urgent	Not Urgent
Important	P1: Tasks P2 P3	P1: Tasks P2 P3
Not Important	P1: Tasks P2 P3	Time wasters Eliminate these tasks

While working on your tasks, be prepared that the first two to three weeks will take the longest. As you progress through the routine in the subsequent weeks or months, this exercise will increasingly take no more than fifteen minutes. Most people find that the best time to do this exercise is late evening before sleeping or early morning. This is also the best time for self-reflection and the time when our mind is seemingly at peace and uncluttered.

As you progress through this daily time management exercise, you will realise that the monthly tasks move to weekly and the weekly tasks move to daily. You will achieve far more than you had initially anticipated. Your productivity levels will soar, and your self-esteem and confidence will scale higher. Most importantly, you will be in control of yourself in your transformation journey. Remember, we cannot control everything around us, but we can control and direct ourselves in the intended direction.

Having defined a time management schedule to ensure you are on the right trajectory, there are ten techniques that you must adopt to effectively manage your time and remain on top of your game.

1. Commit to being organised and develop a sense of purpose and urgency in everything you do. Be sensitive to the lapse of time. Arrive five minutes early for your appointment, not just official ones but also the personal ones. Showing respect for other's time is showing respect for your time. People are quick to reciprocate in the same way. This sets the tone for a productive meeting.
2. Assess your current time spent and build a log to know how you presently spend your time. What are your peak performance hours, and what tasks get addressed during these hours? You need to ensure that your important and urgent tasks are allocated during your peak performance hours.
3. Make time management a way of life and develop it into a habit. Adopt time management tools and mobile apps that will help you capture your activities and manage your tasks based on the priorities set.
4. Allocate time daily to reflect, review, plan, and self-manage yourself.
5. Offload tasks that can be done by your team, family members, and even by friends if they are involved.

6. Do not be lethargic and procrastinate on your critical tasks, like Brian Tracy quotes in his book, *Eat That Frog!*
7. Take time to daily recharge, reenergise, and recalibrate yourself towards your goals by meditating.
8. Stay disciplined to stay focussed. Avoid time wasters both at the office and outside working hours.
9. Follow up with yourself. Understand what roadblocks are preventing you from achieving your important tasks. Are these internal or external blocks?
10. Ensure you review your tasks daily. Strike off the completed tasks and update your list with new tasks to be completed. Write them down daily before you retire for the day.

5.8 Manage Your Health . . . For High Performance

You can't be great if you don't feel great. Make exceptional Health Your #1 Priority

—Robin Sharma

Your body is the transport vehicle in your transformation journey. As individuals lead themselves through the transformation journey, they must not only look and feel good from the outside but also feel great from the inside. While we take care of our mind and soul, we should also care for our body. Your body is like a car engine that runs smoothly when it is well maintained. The more time and effort you invest In looking after your body, the more productive it will be.

Caring for our body means several things besides just health. It means the way we eat, sleep, exercise, groom, and manage our physical environment. The quality of our health plays a key role in the way we feel about ourselves. We feel good about ourselves when our health is good.

When we eat right, we think clearly, act with purpose, and sleep well. The key is to know what to eat, when to eat, and how to eat. Developing healthy eating habits requires discipline and persistence. You must start caring about your body and loving yourself. In order to do that, it must be nourished and maintained regularly.

Maintaining a good state of health will allow you to be resilient and bounce back. It will energise you to take on more tasks required to achieve your goals. Your mind knows what you must do and will drive the energy into the body to get it done. Developing a healthy lifestyle will enable your body to maintain those high energy levels of peak performers.

Start with a few simple steps. Love your body for what it is today, no matter how overweight or underweight you are. Your body is an instrument that plays the music the way it has been played upon. You are responsible for the current state of your body. So take charge of your body today, let go of all past inhibitions, and work on it.

Visualise the target state you want for your body. Add this to your vision board. Relentlessly work on it day after day, week after week, month after month, just as a parent nourishes its child. Yes exactly, you need to respect and treat your body as though it is your child. Give it all the nourishment and enrichment that life can afford you to give it. Keep it healthy and fit for a better tomorrow. Your body is the only thing that will always be with you throughout your life. No one will care about it more than you do.

Exercise:

Here are twelve steps on getting your health back on track by leveraging five simple elements viz. *Water, Air, Food, Exercise, and Sleep*

1. Start with a routine health check to assess the current state of your health. Alternatively, to know your health

status, check your weight on the scale and measure it against your BMI (Body Mass Index).

2. Based on the areas identified by your physician, establish your Health Goals.

3. Develop the daily habit of drinking three to four litres of water a day. Start your day with a glass of warm water to clear the body toxins and end your day with a glass of water before doing to bed to help aid your digestion, blood circulation, and sleep. During the day, drink a glass of water every hour. Water provides incredible benefits in improving your health.

4. Exercise for an hour a day. Start with a daily morning walk for at least thirty minutes and meditating for ten minutes after your walk. Meditate to bring the mind and body to a standstill. The other activities you could include are to take the stairs instead of the elevator, park your car the farthest from the office to ensure you walk more, and make sure to move your body every hour. Target ten thousand steps a day to achieve at least fifty thousand steps a week.

5. Go vegan on the first three working days of the week to detox your body. This will not only boost your energy levels during the week but would also help you to recover from your weekends. Commit to eating fresh foods and fruits.

6. Develop the habit of deep *breathing*. Most people have shallow breaths, but with a conscious approach, you can improve your breathing habits. A simple yet powerful breathing technique will clear your mind and also promote weight loss. To do this tighten your abdominal muscles, breathe in deeply counting zero to three and then breathe

out counting four to ten. Do this three times to clear the
mind.

7. Zero down on all your sugar intake. Reduce your salt
intake to half.

8. Ensure you have seven to eight hours of sleep a day during
the week. There is no right or wrong time to sleep. Having
said that people commonly sleep by 10:00 p.m. and wake
up by 5:00 a.m., thereby giving them seven hours of sleep.
Spend five minutes listing down your daily thoughts just
before you sleep.

9. Planning your next day will allow you to sleep soundly.
Ensure to have your dinner by 7:00 p.m. to allow your body
three hours to digest the food before you sleep.

10. The key to managing your body is to maintain a high
metabolism during the day to burn the excess calories.
Reduce your meal portions to half and have your three
meals between 8:00 a.m. and 7:00 p.m., post which you
can hydrate yourself as needed with water.

11. Promote healthy living with your family, friends, and
colleagues. This puts you in a leadership position to lead
a healthy lifestyle.

12. Ensure that your interactions with people are always positive
and your thoughts are controlled to remain positive. This
will ensure that you avoid negative thoughts, leading to
better health and productivity.

5.9 Build Your Safety Net . . . By Securing Financially

If you don't master money,
it's going to master you.

—Tony Robbins

It is one aspect to inherit financial wealth, and completely another to be financially literate to manage and grow that wealth. There have been individuals, sports personalities, and celebrities who have either earned or inherited their wealth only to lose it due to financial illiteracy, indiscipline, and bad spending habits. They did not have the financial literacy or the awareness to save and invest their wealth for their future. The individuals who have thrived and grown their wealth have been fortunate to either educate themselves financially or build a network of friends who helped them get there. They have learned the art of doing what it takes to enter, remain, and thrive in the high-net-worth individual league. The ones who were ignorant about financial literacy perished and died bankrupt.

For those who have not inherited wealth, you have the choice to become financially literate and build your wealth. You have the opportunity that life presents to you to build your wealth and meet your financial aspirations. You can reach your milestone and leave a legacy for your future generations. You must take the initiative to commit to this journey of building your wealth and securing your future. It is never too late to start, no matter how old you are. If you still earn an income, it is good enough to plan and start your journey towards financial independence.

You must be wondering what has building financial wealth got to do with transformation. Should individuals fail in their transformation journey, they need to make sure that they have a financial safety net that will help them bounce back.

Failures could be due to job losses, companies shutting down, huge medical expense bills that are not covered by insurance, getting trapped with too many financial debts, having a bad debt, making a bad investment decision, . . . the list could go on. Having a financial safety net will help you bounce back faster. Money has the power to make or break you. If you have saved enough funds, then no matter what, you will bounce back with ease. If you do not have enough financial savings, you can still bounce back, only the journey to recovery will be harder and longer.

Your financial wealth serves as a security layer to insulate you from disastrous circumstances and also contributes to your retirement savings. Building your financial wealth is building your safety net. The hard truth is that wealth plays a key role in our life. Financial institutes are available, but individuals should know when and how to leverage their services. Individuals must have their financial base established, relevant to their financial goals and risk appetite.

The stock market, commodity market, real estate market, and other markets have their own operating models and systems.

Gaining an understanding of their operating systems takes time, and it is a long learning curve. Some individuals develop a mental block trying to understand how these markets operate and function. As a result, they remain satisfied withholding their savings safely in bank deposits. Only a small percentage of the world population knows how these markets operate, or what drives the stock exchange index up or down. It is this 1 per cent that makes the money from the rest.

The level of financial inequality around the world continues. Not only do the rich get richer but the smart get richer too. According to the Credit Suisse 2019 report, 44 per cent of global household wealth resides with just 0.9 per cent of the world's population. The rest of the statistics from the chart below are self-explanatory and shocking.

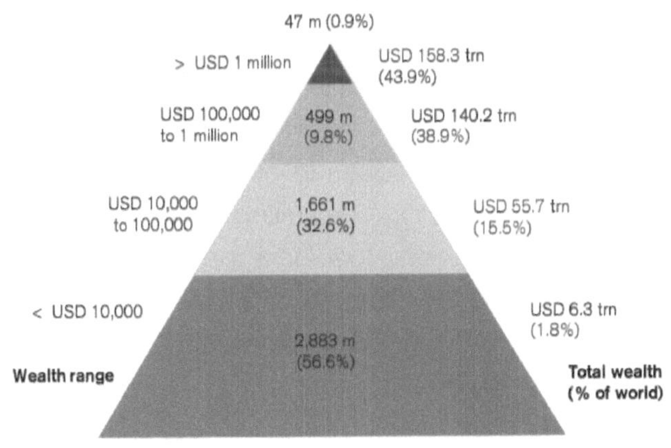

Source: James Davies, Rodrigo Lluberas and Anthony Shorrocks, Global wealth databook 2019

The imperative question for individuals is to know what it would take to be financially independent and at what age. How should the common man start its journey to being financially independent? While there are many financial experts, books, and courses available out there, the secret to building your financial wealth is to "keep it simple and work within your limits."

Exercise:

1. Write down what financial independence means to you.
2. Next, write down the first number that comes to your mind that you believe would make you financially independent. Most people would likely write a million dollars.
3. Decide what you want from your financial plan. Is the objective retirement planning, financial independence, starting a business, or any other? List down your financial goals.
4. Now define the timelines to achieve this. "By When" do you want to have the one million dollars? Do you want to have it in three years, five years, or ten years? Write down "By When" next to the number $1 M.
5. Build an outline of "How you would achieve this?" And who can help you achieve this?

Wealth-building formula

A simple yet powerful wealth-building formula is ESI (Earn To Save To Invest).

Financial Wealth = Earnings + Savings + Investments

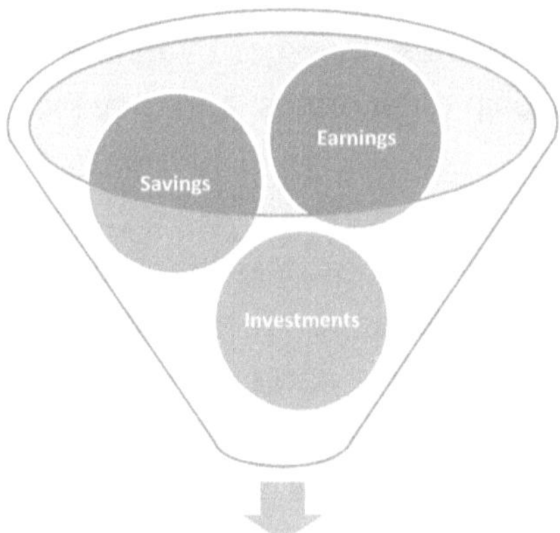

Financial Wealth

Money earned (Earnings) would depend on sources of income, current employment, and how marketable you are in the market. The more marketable you are, the higher are the chances you will earn well. There is no smallness in starting with a low income. There is always a starting point for anyone, as they progress to earn through their careers.

Money saved (Savings) is income (money earned) less expenses (money spent). There are people with a lavish lifestyle who end up spending their monthly income, leaving them with little or nothing for the following month. Their lifestyle continues, as they earn more, they spend even more. They eventually get trapped into a cyclic debt, simply because they spent more than what they earned and, in the process, over-leveraged themselves. Their expenses exceeded their income. Eventually, they drift into more debts to pay for their expenses. They then take more personal loans to pay for previous personal loans. They borrow money from banks, their best friends, and family, promising to pay them back soon. Soon never comes, they get caught into a financial debt trap, their relationship deteriorates, and they lose confidence and drift into isolation.

These individuals drown not only themselves into bad debts but also their family and dependents. These people need help to change their destructive habit of spending. No matter how much an individual earns, if his expenses are not controlled, he would continue to drag his state of poverty, wherever he goes.

The bottom line is you must be frugal in your spending habits and manage your expenses within the income you earn. Every month, you must have a fixed per centage of money saved from your monthly income. There is no quick-fix formula except developing the disciplined habit of saving money by controlling your expenses. Start small if you must but start now!

Most people stop at thinking they have done a great job in saving money. They forget that money saved does not mean much unless it is put to productive use (Investments). The money saved must make money for you and over time must earn you interest on the principal you invested or appreciate the valuation of your assets. Your investments can be into several categories from bank deposits, mutual funds, stocks, real estate, etc. and must appreciate over time.

The more you invest, the more you will earn; the more you earn, the more you must save to invest again. This formula if followed with rigour and discipline will increase your financial wealth and net worth with time.

Emergency fund savings

Money saved must be channelised into various financial investments. The amount of money in each of these streams would depend on your age, earning capacity, risk appetite, current situation, and plans. Financially aware individuals divide their savings into two or more parts. The first significant part is called your *emergency funds*. The emergency funds should be large enough to cover all your ongoing expenses for five months.

1. To know your emergency funds, write all the expenses you incur for the month. These expenses could be rent, EMI (equated monthly installments) on mortgages, electricity, water, groceries, school fees, petrol, etc. Let us say, this adds up to $2,000 per month.

2. Add a 20 per cent contingency to the expenses, so your monthly total is now $2,400 per month. The 20 per cent is your contingency for any unexpected expenses that may surface up.

3. Once you have ascertained this amount, you must then plan your emergency savings for the next five months. You must place in your mind that no matter what happens, you will bounce back within five months. Your emergency fund is now $12,000, i.e., $2,400 per month for five months. This is your baseline emergency funds you must always maintain. As the emergency funds increase over time, it will give you more comfort and peace of mind.

4. Having ascertained your emergency funds, your next task is to work out the amount you can invest. This goes back to the ESI formula (Earn-Save-Invest). Say if your monthly salary was $4,000, your monthly expenses were $2,400 (Including the 20 per cent contingency), you are left with $1,600 ($4,000 minus $2,400) towards savings. Common

sense and experience teach us that we must not spend more than we earn. You should then plan to save $1,600 at the start of the month, for 7.5 months, to build your emergency fund of $12,000.

5. Once the emergency fund target of $12,000 is achieved, it can be tucked away safely into a six-month term, bank deposit with an auto-renewal of the term so you do not have to administer it unless required.

Emergency Funds

Monthly Salary		$4,000 (A)
Monthly Expenses	$2,000	
Add 20% Contingency	$400	
Total Monthly Expenses		$2,400 (B)
Balance Funds		
$4,000 (A) – $2,400 (B)		$1,600 (C)

Emergency Funds for Five Months is $2,400 (B) *5 months	$12,000
Save $1,600 (C) for 7.5 Months	$12,000

Having established your emergency funds, you will achieve a sense of partial independence and relief. The emergency funds must be reviewed every quarter or at any new significant events such as marriage, the birth of your child, change in jobs, relocating to a new place, and more. Rework your emergency funds based on the developments happening in your life.

The second part of your savings is called your *investable savings*. These are savings you plan to invest, after securing your emergency funds. The $1,600 per month that was used to build the emergency funds can now be diverted towards building your investments. There are various options and would depend on what you want to achieve as a financial goal. In case you want to invest in your security, you may opt for life insurance, health insurance, retirement benefit, children's education, and critical illness. If your plans are to grow your wealth, you may want to invest in different asset classes like real estate, stocks, mutual funds, commodity trading, or cryptocurrency, among others. Here are five steps to help you build your plan.

Exercise:

1. Assess what is your current Net Worth. You derive your net worth by totalling all your assets (house market value, gold, investments, emergency funds, short-term savings, bank account balance, etc.) minus your liabilities (mortgages, home loans, car loans, student loans, credit card balances, money borrowed from family and friends, etc.)
    Net Worth = (Assets) – (Liabilities)
2. Reestablish your goals. Some examples include:
    *   Short term: Purchasing a vehicle, annual vacation, etc.
    *   Mid term: Relocation to another country, job change, getting married, etc.
    *   Long term: Retirement, education, own business, etc. Target investment plans for children's education, retirement, life insurance, and health insurance.
3. Decide how much you want to invest each year and for how long. Typically investors would take a seven-to-fifteen-years view to ensure a steady return on their investments.
4. Ascertain your risk appetite. This will largely depend on several factors such as job stability, earning capacity, age, liabilities, and dependents and their age.

5. Finally, target your investable savings. You could evaluate and select various asset classes like real estate, equity, debt, gold, and cash. The distribution of your investments across these asset classes would depend on your age, goals, and risk appetite.

For stocks and mutual funds, if you are aged below thirty-five, you should plan for high equity to debt investment ratio—that is, invest about 80 per cent into equity funds and balance 20 per cent into debt funds. If you are between forty and fifty, then plan for moderate equity to debt ratio—that is 50 per cent into equity funds. If you are above fifty, then plan for low equity to debt ratio and limit your exposure to equity to 20 per cent. As you grow older, you want to make sure you are protecting your principal invested.

Another asset class that has proven itself is real estate. Investments in real estate should start as early as possible. Take a home loan to buy yourself a house, preferably the one you live in to save on the rent. As you settle down in your career, plan to invest more into income-generating real estate (apartment, offices, and shops) within your limits. The idea is to build a real estate portfolio that will eventually generate income to offset part of the mortgages. Once your mortgages are settled, the income generated from your real estate portfolio will add to your retirement income plan.

The monetary investments you make are key to securing your future state of financial independence. So, what does financial independence mean? *In simple terms, it is the state you reach in life when you do not have to work for someone else or yourself for the rest of your life. Your investments earn you income to take care of all your expenses.*

Retirement planning

Most people who have been through the financial planning exercise, perhaps late in their life, will tell you they wished they had started planning first for their retirement. More often than not, people prioritise many other areas such as owning a house, education fund for their children, buying a car, and so on. They tend to give their retirement planning the least priority. Their realisation surfaces when their children have completed their education and are off on their own path. Their ability to save for their retirement now depends on being employed to earn a monthly income, added with their age disadvantage.

They wished they had started planning or saving for their retirement earlier in life, simply because their annual or monthly contribution towards their retirement would be relatively small. Assume you start when you are thirty years old and plan to retire when you are fifty-five years old. This would give you a twenty-five-year window to build your retirement funds.

Let us say you invested $500 per month or $6,000 annually towards your retirement planning for the next twenty-five years. This would be worth $457,420 at an annual compounded interest rate of 8 per cent. This, of course, could easily take you to a $1 million if you were to increase the monthly amount from $500 per month to $1100 per month. This would be the simplest way to retire being a millionaire. A simple step, leveraging the power of compounding interest, would take you into the elite club when you retire.

We all want to attain a state of financial independence. While there are several ways to achieve this, it is crucial that individuals protect themselves when age is not on their side and their earning capacity has slowed down, if not stopped. From speaking to people, we learned that the best earning years for an individual are between forty and fifty years. If he is highly competent and lucky, he could extend that period to sixty or sixty-five years.

With a simple financial plan, you could be in the elite wealth club. You only need the courage to start and be disciplined to stay committed to your financial goals and gain the status of financial independence. It is never too late—start now.

5.10 Build Your Personal Network . . . Be a Propellant

*Success isn't about how much money
you make; it's about the difference
you make in people's lives.*

—Michelle Obama

By now, you should have identified your life purpose and goals, what you need to do to get there, and by when. The next ingredient to add is "who." Who will help you to achieve your goals? The answer to this is "you" and "your network." Leveraging the untapped strength that lies within you and your network will determine the pace of your transformation journey. Higher the leverage, the more effective the outcomes. Your personal network is an asset to you. Yes, literally a financial asset to you. Treat it like one. It could also be a liability depending on the type of friends present in your network.

Life is an ongoing transformation journey. Whether you accept it or not, each day is different from the other, and you subconsciously adapt to each new day. Driven by the universal forces, you will have your high and low phases in the transformation journey. You reach the high phase with the support of your natural allies, viz., your network, knowledge, skills, and competency. When in the low phase, you relaunch with the support of your allies. During the high phase, your network grows in leaps and bound.

Your success becomes the centre of gravity and has a natural gravitational force to attract more people into your network. The net worth of your network is high. At this stage, you are an asset that everyone wants to be associated with.

During the low phase, your success deteriorates and are no longer the centre of gravity. Along with it, your network starts to evaporate, and it tends to lose the earlier momentum and attractional force. People tend to stay low and away from you. At this stage, you are a liability that most people tend to stay away from. The net worth of your network is reduced. You are left with a "residual network," which genuinely values you.

The residual network is your baseline and forms your core network. It is the core to your survival. This is a network of a few people who will stand by you in bad times and in good times. The few people could be in single digits. They have a natural affinity towards you. They unconditionally offer help with no expectations of getting anything in return. They are the safety net for your relaunch.

Exercise:
Do you know who forms part of your core network? List down the names that immediately come to your mind. Are you part of somebody else's core network? Is this core network the same set of resources that could help you relaunch?

No matter what stage and state your current network is, it is paramount that you assess your current position and plot it onto the Active Value grid. The Active Value grid was developed by the author based on his experience of networking with people over the last three decades.

Active Value Grid

Active/Value	New	Passive	Active
High			
Medium			
Low			

The X-axis has the type (new, active, or passive) of active status. *New* is a contact or person that you want to establish a connection with, in pursuit of your stated goals. *Passive* is a contact that you made or met in person or connected over social media but lost touch, resulting in the contact being dormant or inactive. *Active* is a contact you are regularly connected with daily, weekly, or monthly.

The Y-axis has the type (low, medium, or high) of value. "High value" is a contact that provides immediate value to you and can instantly help you complete your tasks to achieve your goals. High-value contacts are great connectors and add value on their own. "Medium value" contacts are great connectors but do not add value on their own. They can connect you to the high-value network and are high-energy, enthusiastic people. "Low value" contacts can neither add value on their own nor can they connect you to the high-value network.

To complete the exercise on the Active Value (AV) grid, do the following:

1. Knowing your life purpose, goals, and aspirations, establish your networking goals.
2. Assess your current position w.r.t. your network.

3. List down the people with whom you need to connect or reconnect to achieve your goals.
4. After prioritising them, plot these contacts on the AV grid. Circle the contacts that are most critical, you must connect, or stay connected.
5. Write down your plan on how you will connect or reconnect with each of these critical contacts.
6. Write down how you will stay connected with them to sustain the relationship.
7. Find common things—friends, group, or interests—or a "common denominator" to initiate the connection. This usually could be someone from your network or common group.

My network net worth

The value of your network is the net worth of your network. The net worth of your network is calculated by a simple formula. This is a formula to guide building the net worth of your network.

My Network Net Worth (NNW) = My Give (MG1) – My Get (MG2)

> *"My Give = Credit" and "My Get = Debit"*
> NNW = MG1 – MG2 *(MG1 should always be greater than MG2)*

My Give is what you as a person give to your network. This is driven by a karmic law of reciprocation. You must keep giving to people to help and support them. The law of reciprocation comes into play, making people obliged to give back to you. This may or may not be from the same person; it could be a person from someone else in your network. Driven by the laws of karma, the more you give, the more you get. Part of My Give is being a connector—a connector who connects his/her network to each other, thereby building a powerful networking mesh. The less you give, the less you get. Start with giving first to people, both inside and outside your network. *"My Give = Credit."*

My Get is what you as a person get from your network. For your network to be active and effective, you should have the opportunity to first serve your network unconditionally, without expecting anything in return. This will move the scale from a low-value/net worth network to the mid-value network. ("My Get = Debit".)

When you achieve this state, the universal karmic forces drive your network to give back to you. When you keep giving to your network, you establish strong credibility. You will receive value from your network without asking for it. This could be a referral for a new business opportunity or new employment opportunity or even to get introduced to a new high-net-worth networker.

A broader debate has been going on: Is there a science to networking or is it a natural inbuilt talent that you either possess or don't? If you possess this talent in your system, then networking would be seamless for you. If you do not possess the natural talent to network, then the skills can be acquired with practice. The key is to align your networking activities to your goals.

Networking skills can be acquired in a structured and progressive manner. We are all born with an inherent ability to connect and engage with people. It is either tapped and leveraged, or it remains dormant waiting to be tapped.

You can build and strengthen your network by adopting the below steps.

1. **Establish Your Networking Objectives**. Knowing your life purpose, list down the objectives you want to achieve from networking.

2. **Networking Goals Should Be SMART.** Your goals should be SMART. They should be Specific, Measurable, Attainable, Relevant, and Time Bound. Your Networking Goals should also be SMART in terms of what *specifically* do you want out of networking. It could be building connections with prospective clients or suppliers; it could be building connections with people with similar interests or young entrepreneurs or angel investors, etc.

   How do you *measure* the success of your networking? It could be several new contacts, it could be a number of people you helped in a month, it could be a number of new referrals you received, etc. It should be *attainable* and not something ridiculous. It should be *relevant* in terms of being aligned with your goals and life purpose. Lastly, your networking goals should be time bound as in connecting with people you want to connect within a predetermined time frame in mind.

3. **Build Your Social Media Presence**. In the digital world, stakes are high and perception matters. The key is building a consistent digital footprint about yourself. This should be done in a planned and structured manner. Blog, LinkedIn, Twitter, and Instagram are some of the tools you could leverage. Establish a social media plan to promote a consistent online brand image about yourself.

4. **Build a Target Profile of Your Network**. In almost all cases, it would be multiple target profiles. These would include family, friends, customers, colleagues, peers from other industries, and more importantly, people you want to network with and are happy to connect with you.

5. **Schedule and Calendar Time to Network**. To grow the net worth of your network, dedicate thirty minutes every day to build and nurture your connections, including on weekends. This would give you about four to six hours of networking every week, which is a significant time invested.

6. **Consolidate Database of Your Network**. This could be as simple as the contacts in your Outlook, business cards you have collected, or personal email addresses. Build a consolidated database of your network and categorise them.

7. **Rekindle the Old Connects**. Based on your networking objectives, reconnect with your inactive contacts. These include your family, friends, college alumni, ex-colleagues, customers, partners, competitors, and suppliers. It would help to email/WhatsApp and follow up with a call to share information relevant to them.

8. **Find a Role Model**. Finding a role model may not be easy, but it is worth the search. These could be people from your work, your alumni, ex-colleagues/boss, or even family members

9. **Join Associations, Clubs, Groups of Relevance**. Network with like-minded people. You will be amazed by the ideas and power of networking you derive from these groups. The learning and knowledge you acquire will be invaluable.

10. **Value Your Time**. As far as possible, have your breakfast, lunch, and dinner with someone; plan to invite someone

even if it is family. Have your meal with a family member when at home, or when at work have your lunch with a colleague, customer, or supplier. You could also include people you know outside your work life with whom you share common interests.

11. **Share Your Knowledge.** One of the powerful ways to both give and create a powerful impact is to present or speak at any given opportunity. This could be planned or extempore. In either case, always have your presentation pitch or talking points ready on your favourite topic.

12. **Stay Current.** This is a great way to break the ice while meeting new people and also to assess and gauge their interests. More importantly, you will easily establish areas of common interest and conversation.

13. **Practice Your Introduction.** Prepare a thirty-second introduction about yourself on who you are and what you do to serve or help people. Write this down in hundred words and practice it aloud till you perfect it.

14. **Engage a Mentor.** A mentor is a specialist in his/her field who can guide you. Reach out to people within your network, and you will be surprised how eager people are to mentor you.

15. **Be a Coach to Someone in Need.** You will be amazed at how effective you could be by lending your time to someone in need.

16. **Referral.** Be generous to share referrals with your connections unconditionally. By the same token, do not be afraid to ask for referrals when you really need one.

17. **Be Honest, Caring, and Transparent.** The one thing people love about meeting new people is the instant

connection they establish. The quickest way to achieve this is to be sincere in your approach. Just be yourself.

18. **Maintain Your Self-Esteem.** No matter how accomplished you are or how unaccomplished you are, the truth remains that the new person you are meeting has no clue about it, in most cases. Hold yourself in high self-esteem, extend a firm handshake, and introduce yourself while looking at the person in the eye with confidence.

19. **Be an Active Listener.** One of the biggest dampeners when you meet someone new for the first time is not getting their active attention when you speak to them. Be an attentive listener when people introduce themselves to you. Lock your posture and eye contact facing the person in front of you, without looking over them or sideward.

20. **Follow Up.** This is probably the most underrated element of networking that is crucial for sustaining your connections. How many times have you forgotten to follow up with a person you met during a conference or met through a common connection? Follow up is an art and needs planning and discipline to execute. Decide in advance the message you want to communicate based on your previous meeting and create a follow-up thread to have a subsequent meeting or even a call.

21. **Be Dressed for the Occasion**. Always be dressed for the occasion. After all, you are your own brand ambassador. How you package yourself will depend on how you want to be perceived. In a *Work from Home* mode, be prepared for video calls. This portrays your professionalism and preparedness to engage and serve.

Invest time to plan, build, and nurture a network. This is an invaluable asset that will give you the returns on your time invested. This is one of the few assets that will serve as your safety net well beyond your retirement age.

Commit to construct and establish your network. Building a quality network takes time and patience. Like a wheel, once it is set in motion, it needs to be regularly stimulated to keep it in motion. Keep tapping into your network, and it will only grow larger and stronger. Be genuine, transparent, and positive in your approach. Follow up regularly to stay connected. Remember, people buy from people they know.

5.11 You Are a Product of Yourself

*Branding is what people say about you
when you are not in the room.*

—Jeff Bezos

Imagine for a moment two different brands of the same product. The first one is a proven, popularly known brand, and the second is a recently launched new brand. They both falter at the same time with the same defect. The product with a powerful brand is better insulated to recover and continue its journey. When a product has a powerful brand, the recovery cycle is quicker. The same is not true when a product with a weaker or unknown brand has a mishap, its recovery would take significantly longer and at times could severely impact the future of that brand.

Higher the brand equity, stronger is the brand perception with a faster recovery time. Lower the brand equity, weaker is the brand perception and slower is the recovery. Powerful brands have been through a journey of building their brand equity by creating strong perceptions.

These behavioural trends of products are driven by consumers and hence are seamlessly applicable to the people themselves. People with high authenticity gain faster trust and reliability. They build a robust brand equity of consistency and are dependable. Their authenticity helps them to win big on perceptions. They are able to scale their personal brand equity at a rapid pace, and their recovery from a mishap is quicker.

As you undergo your personal transformation, building and maintaining your brand equity will insulate you to a large extent from the tremors in your life. You are a product of yourself. This may sound ridiculous at first to believe, but it is true. Just as a product that transcends through the various stages of its life cycle, you transcend through the various stages of your product life cycle (PLC).

I am not a product of my circumstances. I am a product of my decisions.

—Stephen Covey

What is a product life cycle (PLC)?
It is important to understand the product life cycle and how this would fit into an individual product life cycle. A product life cycle has five different stages viz., *Development, Introduction, Growth, Maturity, and Decline.* In the *Development stage,* the product could either be an idea or in the process of being manufactured. In either case, it is not introduced to the market. The product is in the *Planning stage.* During this stage, there are no sales, and only costs are being incurred. It is an expensive stage with anticipation and expectation from the product.

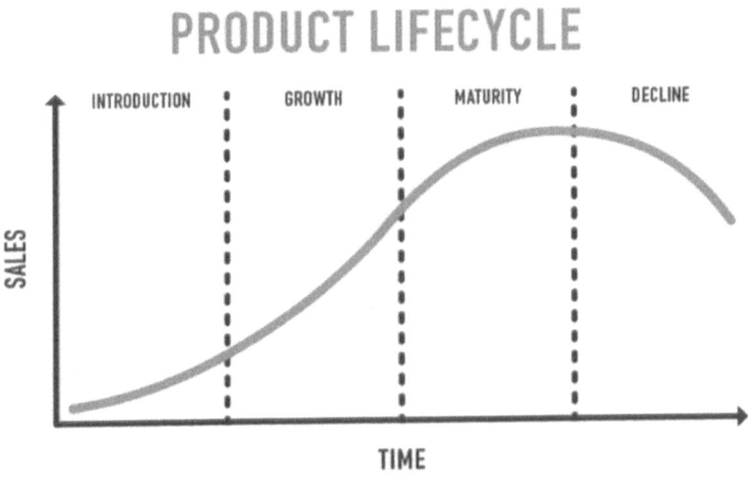

In the *Introduction stage,* the product enters the market, product awareness is low, and the market for the product needs to be developed. The product is relatively new and unknown in the market. During this stage, product sales are low, and costs are still high with a strong focus to generate demand for the product.

In the *Growth stage*, the market becomes aware of the product. The demand for the product increases, sales increase, and costs get offset from the increased sales. Innovative products tend to have an edge and could be priced high, for a longer time. In the *Maturity stage*, sales are the highest, but growth in sales tend to slow down due to the entry of new competitors. The product features need to be regularly upgraded for the product to remain competitive and maintain its market share and position. In this stage, sales for the products could grow, but at a reduced price point. In the *Decline stage,* sales for the product begin to drop, the market is saturated with the product, competition is high, and, more importantly, customers' needs have changed.

If you are wondering what happens to the product after the decline stage—they perish or rise again. The products that perish are the ones that have failed to innovate and transform. Whereas the products that rose again have innovated during the PLC to transform and avoid the decline stage.

Your product life cycle (PLC)

We now extrapolate the PLC to create an individual PLC. Let us look at an individual as a product or brand and how they get plotted onto the product life cycle. Take the instance of an individual's career or employment journey. The first stage would be the *Pre-development stage*. In this stage, the individual focusses on building himself with a specific goal in mind. He is a product of his academics and experiences. His self-belief, self-esteem, and self-confidence get shaped by these experiences. In this stage, individuals identify their goals and what they want to achieve. They understand that creating the right brand image and perception of themselves is paramount.

In the *Development stage,* they decide how they will achieve their goals and who will help them achieve it. In this stage, individuals decide which profession, company, and location they want to target for their jobs. They assess what skills are required to meet the job and role expectations. They invest in building the necessary skills to launch themselves. They take stock of their strengths and how to position themselves in the market. They understand their shortcomings and what needs to be done to manage and mitigate them.

In the *Introduction stage*, the individual approaches the market in search of employment. He understands that his knowledge, experience, and presentability will play a key role in securing a new job. Most entrepreneurs will agree that their personal brand and credibility is crucial for attracting potential investors and customers. Their personal brand helps to build immediate trust in their products and services.

In the *Growth stage*, the individual is being sought out by prospective employers or prospective investors and customers, backed by high market value. Prospective employers want to onboard, and recruiters want to be associated with these individuals.

In the *Maturity stage,* the individual has probably reached his peak in terms of his credibility, performance, and market perception. He is probably earning his highest income. At this stage, the individual needs to maintain his unique competitive advantage, failing which he would get pushed into the decline stage.

At times, they may need to proactively relaunch themselves back to the growth stage of the PLC. This could be by reentering their development phase and progressing to the growth phase.

The key to sustaining your own brand equity is to remain in the development, growth and maturity phases of the PLC. As individuals reach the maturity stage, they need to anticipate well in advance and upgrade or gain new skills that will uniquely differentiate them in the market. They need to take an innovative approach to building their knowledge and competency. They need to invest in both time and money to future-proof their growth and remain focussed on sustaining their growth trajectory.

By orbiting in the growth stage in a consistent cyclical manner, you not only ensure a strong brand equity but also a quicker relaunch when the decline hits you. Your Strong Personal Brand serves as your safety net to relaunch.

5.12 Establish the Personal Brand Called "You"

Building a strong personal brand takes time, effort, and perseverance. People's perception about you is what will determine their buy-in factor. Stronger the perception, higher the buy-in factor. When people trust a product to give them what they want, they will instantaneously purchase it. Deep-rooted trust is established. What people speak about you, in your absence, is a strong measure of your brand. You may not be able to achieve 100 per cent satisfaction, but it is crucial to work on your brand. Living up to your commitments—*say what you will do and do what you say*, should be the motto—will ensure building a dependable brand that is consistent with people's expectations.

Online Presence: You can enhance your brand by building your presence online. Most individuals, if not all, have an established presence online. The key is to build a consistent online presence about your brand. This could be how you project yourself on LinkedIn, Facebook, Twitter, or Instagram. The digital world is capturing and building your digital footprint based on how you comment, like, or post articles on your sites. Smart individuals look at building their online presence through blogs, sharing relevant articles, or intelligently commenting on posts.

You should build your personal brand by attending conferences or joining online groups in your field of interest. Or even conduct presentations at conferences to demonstrate your knowledge as a thought leader. You could attend networking events to speed date and get to know more people in your field of interest. You could blog or post an article on your area of interest.

You would have probably noticed that there are some individuals who are always sought after by competitors and prospective employers. They are marketable, and their names are on top of recruiter's mind. They have a certain uniqueness about them that leaves behind a long-lasting impression on the people they meet. These individuals could be employed or self-employed. In either case, they uniquely brand themselves with their colleagues, customers, suppliers, and family. They understand the impact of personal branding and the role it plays in securing their future.

Building your personal brand equity is like building a bank balance. You can start at any time and build it dollar by dollar. This amplifying force helps your personal brand reach unprecedented levels and opens a world of new opportunities for you.

Bridging personal branding to personal transformation
What is the *role of personal branding in a transformation journey*? A transformation journey like any other journey has highs and lows. When things go right, you reach a new high, but when they do not, you touch a low. The impact of the lows cannot be predicted. It is your personal brand that propels you higher or that serves as a safety net to help you bounce back.

Transformations are successful when they are led with the right leadership skills. This applies while leading teams as well as while leading yourself. While the leadership ingredients are the same, the propensity of the ingredients may vary. Leading yourself needs higher inner characteristics viz., self-discipline, self-motivation, self-confidence, persistence, and more. Leading a team needs problem-solving, decision-making, delegation, providing directions, etc., besides the characteristics of leading oneself.

For personal transformation to happen, you must start with internalising the journey while wholeheartedly embracing it. When this is in harmony with your life purpose and goals, your journey will be seamless. There are several qualities that come into play on a transformation journey. This could be the transformation of one self or a team. This could be in our personal lives at home or in our professional lives at work.

A father could be relocating to a new country to start his new job. A strong personal brand helped him secure a new job. He must now lead not only himself but also his family. A young lady has got promoted to a higher position at work and now leads a team. Her strong personal brand helped her get a promotion. She undergoes a transformation in taking up the new responsibilities while also leading the team.

In an individual's transformation journey, the key is to manage their emotions as they experience various levels of emotions in their transformation process.

Emotional Intelligence: American psychologist Daniel Goleman helped to popularise emotional intelligence. In his theory, he listed five key elements viz., Self-awareness, Self-regulation, Motivation, Empathy, and Social Skills. Each of these attributes is key to increasing emotional intelligence. Self-awareness is key to understanding your emotions and not letting your emotions rule over you. Individuals must be aware not only of their emotions but also how they react to people and situations. Knowing their strengths and weaknesses, they must trust their intuitions.

At the core of personal brand management is self-leadership. The art of leading yourself before, during, and after the transformation journey is key to building a strong personal brand. Your own brand perception is valued by your self-esteem. The higher your self-esteem, the higher will be the value perception of your brand. When you put a high value on your brand, others will do the same and vice versa. The high-value personal brand must be backed by knowledge, skills, and execution. In building your self-esteem, attitude is everything. The can-do attitude to address any or all situations is key to solving problems and adapting to change. Our attitude is controlled both by our thoughts along with our core and secondary value system.

Executive presence

In building and managing your personal brand, executive presence gives you an immense edge, especially in face-to-face meetings. The packaging is what is what attracts customers to a product. This is what attracts a strong personal brand. Packaging personal brands involves not only the external features but also having the charisma or executive presence.

When you meet someone for the first time, you have already formed your opinion about this individual in the first thirty to sixty seconds. The way an individual carries himself/herself, and the way they are groomed, speak, listen, present their case, and their knowledge on their subject get captured, which either wows or leaves you with a mediocre perception about this individual.

Investing in a few basics will take you a long way in wowing your audience. These include thorough preparation prior to your meeting. This is in terms of researching about the person you are going to meet, reading up on the topic of discussion, listing the talking points for the meeting, clearly defining objectives you want from this meeting, and outlining what a successful meeting would look like for you. Arriving five minutes before the meeting is not a sign of weakness, like some people think. It is an act of professionalism and respect. It gives the other person an instant perception of the value you hold for yourself, for them, and for each other's time.

A thank-you note capturing the key points and follow-up action within twelve hours of your meeting demonstrate your professionalism. It is a great way to thank someone for the time they have invested in meeting you. People want to deal with people whom they perceive to be successful and positive. Packaging yourself to build your personal brand remains central to your brand.

You must always look and dress for your future self. Invest in three formal suits, a few shirts, a tie, a pair of shoes that fit you well, a watch, and a pen. You may extend this by having a branded pen, wallet, and watch. And not forgetting well-groomed hair and looked-after hand nails.

Be genuine, be empathetic, and be yourself always.

Chapter Six

Phase 4—Measure and Monitor

If you can't measure it, you can't improve it.

—Peter Drucker

6.1 Need to Measure

The previous phase on Transformation outlined the steps an individual must adopt to transform themselves. While individuals undergo transformation, there is a natural tendency to get overwhelmed and lose sight of their end goals and objectives.

In a transformation journey, individuals get redefined over the course of their journey. There are several attributes that must be managed and driven together in order to progress forward. Attributes from within ourselves and attributes from our external ecosystem. These attributes can be controlled, depending on whether they are internal or external. For those attributes that cannot be controlled, individuals can track these ahead of time, prepare themselves, and proactively respond to their situation.

The key to successfully managing a transformation journey is the discipline and rigour to continuously monitor and measure progress, while proactively responding. The next time you watch a football or basketball game, observe how the players respond to their general practice vis-à-vis a competitive game. The general practice is played without keeping a score with players from both sides taking a casual approach to the session. The moment the competitive game is played, the lethargy is replaced by a newfound motivation to win. The same principle applies to real life. The moment you keep a score of what you need to do, the auto mode inside you gets triggered with the desire to win and meet your goals. You tend to complete your tasks on time or ahead of time.

Without having measures in place, an individual would have no clue how far they have progressed and how much more needs to be done to reach their milestone. Measures are needed to tell them how they are progressing to meet their goals and objectives.

Measuring progress has a subtle yet powerful effect to enable individuals to transform. At a glance, it will let the individual know how far they have progressed, and, importantly, they will know their *Delta* or the variance, to reach their goals.

Knowing your progress will serve as a powerful motivator for you. It motivates you to work harder towards the accomplishment of your goals. Your mind will work ingeniously to know whom to reach out to, what needs to be done, and how to go about completing the remainder of your tasks.

You get a sense of what resources you require to complete the tasks. Should you lack in these required resources or skill sets, your mind subconsciously thinks out of the box to identify who else, with the required skill sets, could help you complete the tasks at hand.

The momentum gained from measuring progress activates a strong reinforcement to drive you in the right direction. You will also gain self-confidence and self-esteem. Your energy levels soar to unprecedented levels, driving higher levels of productivity. You become result-oriented, rather than just being task-oriented.

Undergoing transformations mandates continuous measurement of your progress. The need is driven by managing the controllable factors as well as being prepared for the uncertainties or factors which are beyond control.

Having got a view on the need to measure progress, the next section addresses how do we measure it.

6.2 How to Measure

The true measure of any business leader or manager is performance.

—Brian Tracy

There are several ways to measure progress. The preferred way to measure may vary from one individual to another. The corporate world has used several tools to measure progress. No matter which tool is used, the underlying objective is to ensure that the tasks, activities, measures, and goals are aligned with your vision and life purpose. This will ensure that the process of measuring progress is a seamless activity, making it an integral part of your daily routine and not a burdening task that must be completed.

At the initial stage, it takes self-discipline to start and perseverance to keep at it. By developing the habit of regularly measuring your progress and linking your scorecard to your objectives, you will be in control and proactively prepared to take the corrective steps ahead of time.

Balanced Scorecard

The *Balanced Scorecard* is one of the widely used tools in the corporate world to measure and manage performance. This was originally developed by **Robert Kaplan and David Norton** with initial participation from *Art Schneiderman*. Kaplan and

Norton have a published article in *Harvard Business Review*, and published a book in 1996 titled *The Balanced Scorecard*.

While the Balanced Scorecard (BSC) is used in the corporate world, there is no reason why it cannot be adopted by individuals in their personal lives. Extending the Corporate Balanced Scorecard to *Individual Balanced Scorecard* (refer the template in this section) and building it block by block will enable individuals to measure their progress while being aligned with their life purpose, goals, vision, and mission.

At the core of the Balanced Scorecard is the vision and mission statement. The vision and mission statements are established in full alignment with the life purpose. These statements guide the individual and remind them of the purpose of their end destination. It not only helps in establishing alignment of the goals and objectives but also serves as a reminder to take the necessary action in a timely manner.

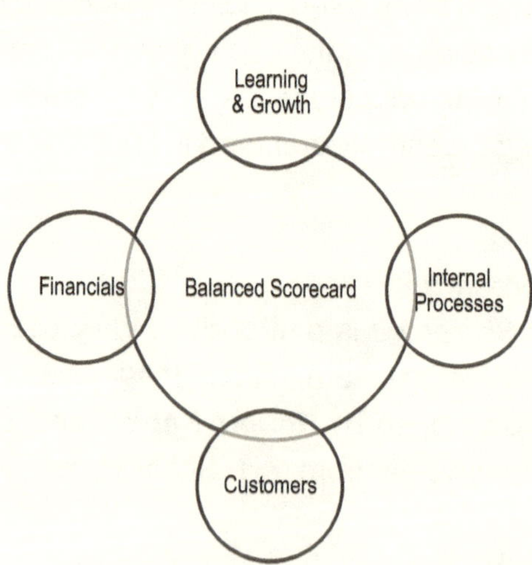

The Balanced Scorecard has four perspectives. These are *Learning and Growth, Internal Processes, Customers, and Financial.* The order of how they are stacked would depend on what is core to the individual. For a student, *learning and growth* would be the foundation pillar, whereas for a salesperson, *customers* would be the foundation pillar. For an individual in an operational role, managing *internal processes* would be the foundation pillar, whereas *finance* would be the foundation pillar for a person in a financial role.

Let us dwell deeper into what drives the four perspectives for an individual. Our digital lives today are being driven by the continuous change and disruption around us. At the core of this change is the ability to quickly adapt to disruptions happening around us. The pace of the disruption cannot be predicted; it would depend on the adoption. An ongoing thirst for knowledge and skills is paramount to survival, and this thirst must be quenched through *Learning and Growth.* Growth comes naturally through learning, and with learning comes knowledge. The digitalised economy was built on the top of the knowledge economy, and it is the key to survival.

The digitalised economy or new age economy has created new roles and new jobs while making some of the existing roles redundant and nonexistent. The redundancy is driven by the need to automate mundane or routine tasks and replace them with automated systems driven by artificial intelligence, machine learning, and robotic automation. Organisations are driven by the need to keep their costs low while increasing their revenues. They are left with no choice but to keep pace, while automating their routine tasks. This allows them to create new roles driven by the new age digital market.

The key to survival for individuals is learning and growth. With the low cost of penetration and commoditized reach of the Internet, gaining knowledge is within everyone's reach. It is up to the individual to reach out, grab it, acquire it, and finally leverage it to her or his benefit.

Having laid the foundation of learning and growth, the key is to be consistent in sustaining it. Consistency can be achieved by ensuring the right habits are cultivated to manage yourself. Self-management is about managing an individual's *Internal Processes*. The way they set goals, review them, control their thoughts and mind, discipline themselves, and manage their time will decide how well they manage their internal processes. Internal processes focus on your execution skills driving higher efficiency and productivity, thereby enabling you to complete the tasks required to achieve your goals.

We deal with several people in our daily lives. Little do we realise that each one of them is a *Customer* to us in some way or the other. These are the people who build and establish an individual's brand equity and form the external perception about you as a person. The internal perception is what you think about yourself, which determines your self-esteem. The better the perception people have of you, the better will be your brand equity.

At your workplace, these people would include your manager, colleagues, and subordinates. In the marketplace, these people would include your customers, suppliers, and partners. At home, this would include your family and friends. You could go a step further and include your ex-colleagues and your alumni.

All these people are the cumulative sum of your customer NPS (Net Promoter Score). How you interact and manage them will determine how high your customer NPS score is. A higher NPS would also strengthen your network, giving you an edge over others in your transformation journey. They would provide you access not only to a wealth of their own resources but also to their networks.

The fourth perspective is *Finance*. This perspective is built on how well you manage your finances. You are the owner and the CEO of "My Inc.," a company owned and managed by you. The state of your financials will determine the fate of your future. Your survival in the real world depends on how financially independent you are and how fast you reach there. If your priority is to grow your investment portfolio, you need to save more to invest more. At some point, you would need to earn more to support your growing responsibilities. To earn more, you would need to change roles or jobs for a senior position. This would depend on your competency, skills, track record, and network.

The four perspectives, Learning and Growth, Internal Processes, Customers, and Financials, could have dependencies on each other or be linked to drive the desired outcome. Having understood the four perspectives of the balanced scorecard, we move to the next step of establishing the strategic objectives of each perspective. A strategic perspective should be easily measurable and not be more than ten or fifteen in number.

Refer to the Individual Balanced Scorecard template at the end of this section.

Your Strategy Map

As an individual, the strategic objectives for the *"Learning and Growth"* perspective could be to increase knowledge, acquire new skills, and improve self-esteem. The strategic objectives for the *"Internal Processes"* perspective could be to improve time management, increase a sense of urgency, or increase the frequency of goal review. The strategic objectives for the *"Customers"* perspective could be to increase the quality of time spent with families and friends, improve customer relationships, improve networking skills, and increase the frequency of business lunches or dinners. The strategic objectives for the *"Finance"* perspective could be to increase earning, reduce expenses, and increase savings. Whatever they are, list them down.

Having listed down the strategic objectives for each **Individual Balanced Score Card (IBSC)** perspective, you could cluster them into strategic themes to bring in a laser focus for each strategic theme. The strategic objectives are linked together where one objective could have a link to another. Achieving one objective would lead to achieving another objective.

For each strategic objective, you need to define a measure. If you wanted to acquire new skills, your measure could be three new skills in a year. If you wanted to improve your time management, your measure could be the number of P1 (Priority 1) tasks completed in a day. If you wanted to improve your network, your measure could be the number of conferences attended or the number of new and reactivated connections made monthly. If you wanted to reduce personal expenses, your measure could be the percentage reduction in monthly expenses.

Measures are established for each strategic objective to enable you to track and monitor how you are progressing on each objective. It helps you to objectively measure the strategic objective. With the measures in place, you list a target for each measure. Measuring progress against the target will immediately tell you how far you have progressed and how much more must be done to achieve your target, for that objective and perspective.

Having worked on the above steps, you have now built an **Individual Strategy Map (ISM)**. This individual strategy map will help you progress on the four perspectives, keeping your vision and mission at the centre stage. Each perspective will be driven by the achievement of the respective strategic objectives.

The *Strategy Map* and *Balanced Scorecard* must be measured at regular intervals. This would be weekly, fortnightly, monthly, or quarterly. The more critical and impactful an objective, the higher should be the frequency to measure. If your objective to reduce personal expenses is at a critical stage, you would need to shift it from a monthly review to a weekly review and even a daily review of your expenses. Tracking and managing your daily expenses will allow you to reach your weekly target and thereby your monthly target.

Some objectives would need to be measured monthly, driven by external factors. If your networking objective is attending seven conferences in a year, then your measure could be monthly or quarterly. It is effective and productive to schedule a weekly self-review of your strategy map. This could be a thirty-minute review on the status of your strategy map.

*Refer to the **Individual Strategy Map** template below.*

Individual Strategy Map (ISM)

Individual Strategy Map for _________________   Date___________

Vision Statement

Mission Statement

Customers
C1 C2 C3

Learning & Growth	Internal Processes
L1 L2 L3	I1 I2 I3

Financial Management
F1 F2 F3

Next Review Date ________________

Individual Balanced Scorecard (IBSC)

Name _________________________   Date _________

Perspective	Strategy	Goals	Objectives	Measure	Target
Customers					
Employees					
Internal Processes					
Financials					

Next Review Date _____________________

Analyse to improve your performance

There are several ways in which you can analyse the data collected on your performance. Adopt the simplest and fastest way that fits you. For instance, athletes feed in their goals, current state, and aspired state into a mobile app. They then use the data collected by their mobile app to analyse their performance and plan their future activities accordingly.

For individuals, depending on your objectives such as weight loss, financial planning, travelling, and learning, there are several options out there. Pick a mobile app that is easy to use and helps you get started quickly. You could even start simple by using a paper and pen to capture and track. The key is to analyse the data on your performance, to track your progress. This activity should be a ritual that you undertake daily, weekly, or monthly. The more you analyse your data, the better understanding you will have on how you have been progressing. When the conscious mind is fed with analysed data, the subconscious mind automatically knows what needs to be done and gets into an execution mode.

There is a correlation between analysis and improvement. In the *first phase*, as you begin to analyse data on your performance and compare it with your baseline plans, you will identify many areas of improvement. In the *second phase*, as you continue to analyse your data, your areas of improvement will reduce largely due to the continuous analysis cycles; The inefficiencies get eliminated and you operate at higher efficiencies. In the *third phase*, the areas of improvement are much lower than the number of analysis cycles. This is the optimal stage when you have reached high efficiencies. You know you are in control of your performance and your progress is on track to completing your planned milestones.

6.3 Monitor Your Environment

Continuously monitoring and measuring progress will enable you to know your current status and the gap to fill your target. Importantly, you will know what needs to be done to fill the gap. What you need to do will be determined by the state of internal and external factors influencing your transformation journey.

Internal factors would include your attributes such as self-leadership, self-management, competency, knowledge, and skills. *External factors* would include markets, industry, geographic location, competition, technologies, new products, new customer needs, and economic and political status. Monitoring both the internal and external environment is crucial to proactively prepare and address any unforeseen disruptions to your transformation journey.

PESTLE
External factors can be monitored in a structured approach. A commonly used tool is PESTLE (Political, Economic, Socio-Cultural, Technology, Legal, and Environmental factors). Use the tool to scan your external environment, and brainstorm to understand the changes happening in each of the PESTLE components.

Some of the questions that can be answered using PESTLE are:

- Is there a new taxation structure that will impact your earnings?

- Is the unemployment rate increasing or decreasing?
- Are there any employment patterns for different age groups?
- Are there new technologies that will have a direct impact on your job, role, and company?
- Are there any legal laws being introduced that could affect the employment of expatriates?
- Is there a shift to adopting eco-friendly solar-powered appliances?

This structured exercise will lead to detecting opportunities and threats driven by each of these changes.

A change in technology could have a disruptive impact on an individual in his workplace. Take, for example, scanning for new technology changes led to knowing that a new automation technology is about to be launched. And this could impact your industry and your job in the next three months. You get a sense of what to expect ahead of time. You could assess if this change provides you with an opportunity or is it a threat. It depends on your perspective and how you proactively respond to this change. A few months later, on scanning your work environment (internal), you learn that your company has decided to implement this new automation technology to improve cost efficiencies and customer satisfaction.

Had you proactively responded to this technological change ahead of time, by acquiring the required knowledge and skills, you probably would have identified an opportunity for a change in a role and got it, as opposed to being vulnerable in your new role at work. You could have also viewed this technology as an opportunity and made yourself marketable for an external job change. By proactively scanning and responding, you could have gained from an external change.

PESTLE is an effective tool when used in conjunction with SWOT. It feeds into the Opportunities and Threats of SWOT. You could extend this to your work and home environment. A classic example of this is Ryan's World Toys review on YouTube with over twenty million subscribers. Ryan, like every other child, loves to play with toys. The parents of this young child saw an opportunity to monetise his interest in toys. They proactively responded to their child's interest and capitalised the opportunity that lay in front of them. Their speed to respond and support their child's interest paid off. Today Ryan is a multimillionaire and the host of a popular toy review channel on YouTube.

Regularly scanning both your internal and external environments would enable you to detect disruptions, like an early warning system. This needs to be done at regular intervals backed by a proactive response to that opportunity or threat.

6.4 Manage Risks to Mitigate

A transformation journey offers several benefits and rewards to an individual, but this does not come without risks. Like most things in life, if we plan well and manage risks to mitigate their impact, the outcome in all probability will be a successful one.

While we measure progress and scan the environment, we must proactively identify risks well ahead of time. Risks could either be perceived or real, based on the data and information we have in hand. Taking a structured approach to managing risks helps to address them in an effective manner, while allocating the right resources to mitigate them.

For instance, an individual taking a reactive approach to an uncategorised risk responds by allocating his best resources to it only to later realise it was a low-risk category. Probably this would leave the individual with scarce resources to allocate for a high-risk category. There is a natural human tendency to reactively manage risks based on past experiences. This jeopardises the individual's efforts to complete their tasks and achieve their goals as planned.

Managing risks involves minimising the probability of things going wrong. The key to managing risk is first to "categorise" them followed by "quantifying" them. This can be achieved by plotting the risks on a "Control–Impact matrix," where the *Ability to Control Risk* is on the Y-axis and the *Potential Impact of the Risk* is on the X-axis.

Based on where the risks are plotted, actions can be planned to mitigate the risk. The key focus should be on Critical Impact—No/Low Control and Major Impact—No/Low Control

Potential Impact		Minor	High	Major	Critical
Ability to Control Risks	No Control				
	Low Control				
	High Control				
	Full Control				

For instance, an individual with the possibility of being made redundant at work is a "major potential impact" for him. Depending on his employment options in the market or potential new roles with his current employer, this could be in "low to high control." The individual must act swiftly on anticipation of being made redundant.

Your sales team member has decided to quit while leading a key deal. This risk is a major potential impact; the ability to control would depend on the backup options and involvement of other stakeholders in the deal itself. The key is to identify and map the risk into the impact–control matrix, based on which appropriate actions can be proactively taken.

The parallel activity to mitigating risk is to quantify them. Quantifying risks can be subjective and biased, based on past experiences and current circumstances. Each risk is different from other risks and hence needs to be assessed before acting on them.

Risks can be quantified based on the *Impact–Probability Matrix*, where the Probability of the risk occurring is on the Y-axis and the Impact of the risk occurring is on the X-axis. Consider this situation where you are in the final stages of closing a business opportunity with one of your key customers. You learn that the Chief Procurement Officer (CPO) is relocating for a better opportunity. Having worked with the CPO for the last eighteen months on the deal, the risk of losing the deal is high. In this case, the Impact of the risk occurring is high and the probability of the risk happening is high too. You need to act immediately to mitigate the risk by leveraging your other management connections with the client,` probably the CEO, CFO, CHRO, CPO, or CIO.

<table>
<tr><td rowspan="2">Probability of Risk Occurring</td><td>High</td><td>**Minimise**
High Risk, but Impact is small. Reduce likelihood of Risk occurring.</td><td>**Danger**
Risk is high and Impact is significant.
Immediate Action.</td></tr>
<tr><td>Low</td><td>**Monitor**
Risk and Impact are low. Monitor for change.</td><td>**Minimise**
Risk is unlikely but Impact is significant. Prepare Plan B.</td></tr>
<tr><td></td><td></td><td>Low</td><td>High</td></tr>
<tr><td colspan="4" align="center">Impact of Risk Occurring</td></tr>
</table>

Quantifying the risk enables you to decide what kind of action is required and the intensity of the action. If the probability of the risk occurring is low and the impact of the risk is high, your action would be to monitor the risk closely and be prepared to proactively respond.

For instance, a crucial senior management meeting between your customer and your company has been scheduled. The probability of the meeting getting canceled is low, but the impact is high. You need to be proactively prepared by reconfirming the meeting well ahead of time and checking if all the attendees have confirmed their attendance and accepted the meeting invite. By proactively responding, you would ensure the meeting happens even if one of the attendees drops out at the last minute.

6.5 Know Your Delta

*I've failed over and over and over again in my life,
and that is why I succeed.*

—Michael Jordan

The key to managing progress is to track and monitor your "delta." Your delta is the difference between what was planned and your actual performance to date. To have a fair assessment of your delta, it is the difference between your Year to Date (YTD) Plan and Year to Date (YTD) Performance. If your overall plan to reach your goals is in ten months and you are in your sixth month, then your delta should be measured as per the sixth month of the YTD plan against your YTD performance in the sixth month.

Individuals are inclined to measure their current performance against the complete plan. They tend to get overwhelmed by the delta that they need to address and at times get demotivated to follow through with the rest of the plan. The key is to know the type of delta you need to measure and how this delta must be addressed.

Delta 1

The YTD Delta (Delta 1) is the difference between YTD Plan vs. YTD Actual. This delta tells you how much you have progressed as of date against your plan. If the delta is measured positive, then you are ahead of your plan. If the delta is measured negative, then you are behind your plan.

The measure is used to know your progress at a given point in time. It is a review of how far you have progressed into your plan. What went right in executing your plan to date, and what did not go right. What resources helped you reach this point of the plan; what knowledge, skills, and competencies were used; did any external factors slow your progress down? It is a true tracking of what your performance should be against your plan. What you should have delivered as of that point.

You may find that the delta is neither positive nor negative. This is a state of perfection, and you need to learn from this. You need to understand what went right and how to sustain the best practices of what you did to reach this state.

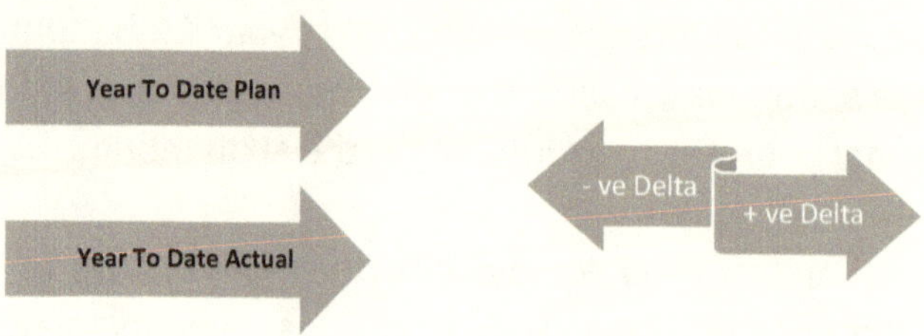

Delta 2

The Overall Delta (Delta 2) is the difference between your Complete Plan and the YTD Actual. This delta tells you what needs to be done to complete the balanced plan. It gives you a view of the journey ahead. At times, the delta may be significant; this is perfectly fine and is likely to happen in the early stages of your plan. As you progress through your plan, the overall delta gets smaller and smaller. The key is to focus on what needs to be done, how you will do it, and the resources needed to support you.

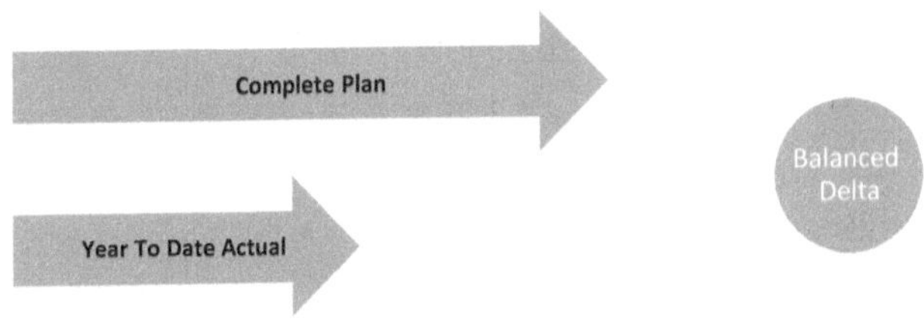

Delta intensity

In your transformation journey, knowing the intensity of the delta will enable you to plan your future course of action. The intensity of the delta could be minor or major. Minor delta is based on the minor variation between the YTD Plan and YTD Actual. When the YTD Actual is significantly higher or lower than the YTD Plan, the delta is major.

Let us say in preparation for your new role, the goal was to acquire new skills at work in the next six months. Five months into the plan, you are yet to progress from Level 1 to the next level of skill acquisition. The delta for this goal is major. If this was your progress, say two months into your plan, then it would be a minor delta.

Measuring the delta intensity

Measuring the intensity of the delta will enable individuals to know what kind of delta they are up against. It serves as an eye-opener to the individuals to understand how they are progressing, what are the potential risks, and how will they activate a recovery plan.

Knowing the truth hurts, but there is nothing better than knowing the truth at the right time, which could help you take the necessary remedial actions and avoid disastrous outcomes. Knowing the delta is like diagnosing the state of your health. The delta must be measured at regular intervals. The frequency of the measures will help in understanding the type and intensity of the delta. The earlier the delta is measured, the easier it is to manage the delta.

At times, individuals tend to inadvertently believe they are ahead of the curve. While this could be true, without having a regular measure for their progress, complacency sets in. They begin to lose their momentum slowly but surely. They begin to fall behind their plans, and by the time they know it, their delta is in a negative state.

The way to ensure that you achieve your goals on time every time is by continuously measuring and monitoring your progress. The results will speak for themselves. They will either motivate you to continue your path in the right direction, or they would raise your anxiety levels and force you to take the corrective actions to catch up with the backlog of the negative delta.

Measuring progress subtly brings in the high level of awareness that feeds into your intuition in addition to your other sources of data. They activate the natural instincts within the individual, enabling them to be aware and proactively respond to changes happening within and outside their ecosystem.

Status–Impact Matrix

The deltas can be mapped on to a Status–Impact Matrix to position them and gauge their impact. On the X-axis is the Impact (Low, Moderate, and High) and on the Y-axis is the Status (Positive and Negative).

The delta is positive when your achievement is ahead of your plans. The delta is negative when your achievement is behind your plans. The delta intensity will vary depending on the impact of your progress and achievements. The matrix will help to plot and categorise your delta, giving you an insight into the impact of the risks that lie ahead and trigger a plan to mitigate those risks.

Status	Impact Delta Matrix		
+ve			
-ve			
Impact	Low	Moderate	High

Next, write down what actions must be taken depending on the delta type. If the delta is -ve and the impact is major, you need to immediately rework your action plan to catch on the lost time. If your delta is -ve and there is no impact, you need to look at the important tasks to be completed, which are not urgent now.

Chapter Seven

Phase 5 — Relaunch

*Our greatest weakness lies in giving up . . . so
never give up, you owe it to yourself to get back
on track and complete the race of life.*

—Albert Einstein

7.1 Manage Your Delta to Retain Control

Knowing your delta helps in understanding the progress made to date or the work that must be done to achieve your goals. The Status–Impact Matrix once completed will provide you with the actions that must be undertaken to improve your delta. Having measured your progress and defined the type of delta, the next step is to manage the delta to relaunch yourself.

Managing your delta involves controlling not only your delta but also your overall progress. With your original plans as the baseline, you need to focus on controlling your progress to control the delta. This would involve taking specific actions to improve your performance and contribute towards reducing the delta.

When your planned tasks are incomplete (-ve delta), you need to identify the gaps and take specific actions to improve your delta. You need to manage your tasks to complete them within the stipulated timeline. If you lack certain specific knowledge and skills required to complete critical tasks, then take control of the situation by reaching out to people who can support you. All tasks related to this -ve delta must move into their Urgent/Important quadrant. These tasks are not only important to address but they are now urgent. Completion of all these pending and current tasks becomes imperative to regain lost ground. You need to work like a firefighter dousing a fire to bring your progress back on track.

When your planned tasks get completed ahead of time or as planned (+ve delta), then you must do everything possible to stay ahead of your plan and maintain a positive delta. The key to your success is consistency. It is like running a race ahead of the other runners. Once you are ahead of your plans, you must remain consistent to keep that lead. The momentum gained from the past progress must be sustained to help you reach your end goal.

The Status–Impact Matrix has six quadrants in total. If your status is negative, then check the appropriate quadrant to map your impact. If your position is in Quadrant 1 then proactive detection of potential future hurdles and planned resolutions will help maintain your progress. If your position is in Quadrants 2 or 3, the focus should be to accelerate efforts, develop a sense of urgency, complete the high- and medium-priority tasks, and immediately reach out for help. Focus all your efforts on catching up with the backlog to prevent further deterioration in progress. Execution and follow up are the key elements; delegate where possible and directly manage the critical activities that have a high dependency.

Status	Status–Impact Delta Matrix		
+ve	4	5	6
-ve	1	2	3
Impact	Low	Moderate	High

For Quadrants 4, 5, and 6, the key is to proactively measure the impact. This is normally a temporary state, and the key is not to let complacency set in as this could easily result in a negative delta or slipping into Quadrants 2 or 3. The focus should be on continuous improvement and consistent performance.

The State—Level Transforming Matrix

While relaunching, individuals must be prepared to progress simultaneously not only in one direction but across the three states. The state and level matrix will help individuals to plot their level by state, depending on the progress made.

Timeline	Timeline	Timeline	
Levels	State 1	State 2	State 3
L3			Transformed State
L2	Transformation	Transformation	
L1	Work as Usual		
L0		Work as Usual	

Level 0 and Level 1 refer to their work as usual (WAU). The industry term for WAU is "business as usual" (BAU). Level 2 is transformation in motion. L3 is the transformed state. States 1, 2, and 3 are the different stages an individual experiences across their transformation journey.

In State 1, the focus is on launching transformative initiatives while maintaining the WAU—work as usual status quo. The key is to proactively prepare for the *Transformation* ahead of time while retaining 80 per cent focus on *Work as usual*.

In State 2, the focus is to execute and adopt the transformation changes. The progressive shift is from work as usual to transformation. Having successfully tried and tested the transformational initiatives, they are moved into adoption where the individual starts to apply and fully adopt new transformation initiatives.

State 3 is the final transformed state where the planned transformation is complete. The progressive shift from *work as usual* is complete and transitioned, thereby leading them to a transformed state.

Take an example of a young, fresh graduate who has just started working and has a great idea with plans to launch his new start-up. Does he stop everything and jump straight into his start-up? Absolutely not! He should continue to work as usual with his current employer, while acquiring the necessary experience, knowledge, and skills. On weekends, he could build his business plan and work out the resources required. When he is fully ready, he can shift 100 per cent from his day-to-day job to fully launch his start-up.

7.2 The "X" in "ReLaunch X"

The kaizen philosophy assumes that our way of life—be it our working life, our social life, or our home life—deserves to be constantly improved.

—*Masaaki Imai*

The word "kaizen" in Japanese means continuous improvement. The continuous improvement process requires one to analyse their performance, understand the root causes, learn how to improve, and take the necessary steps for improvement. This can be applied across all aspects of an individual's life. The process of continuous improvement if mapped onto a graph would resemble the infinity symbol as depicted below, where the performance analysis and associated root cause cycle loop back and feed into the improvement and execution cycle.

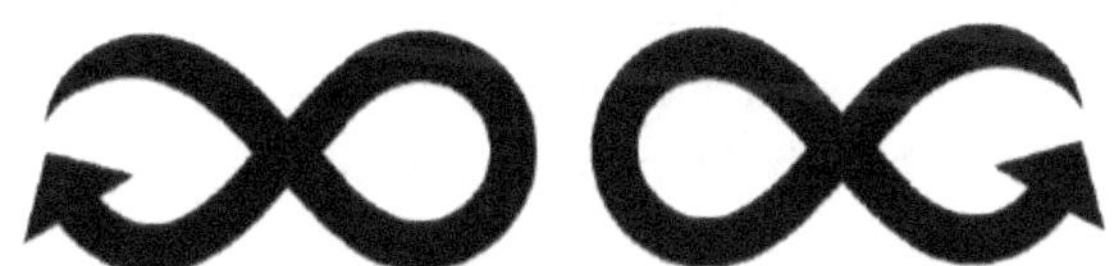

The Continuous Improvement Loop.

In the previous chapters, we covered the delta and how to manage it. The delta is like a valuable stone; if it is refined and cut with precision, it will turn out to be your gemstone. The skill to cut a raw gem with precision is accumulated over time and after multiple iterations of learning. The learnings from each cutting session are fed into the next cutting session. The cutting skill evolves from beginner to intermediate to expert level. The delta on its own is a raw stone; it depends on how it is leveraged not once but multiple times in a continuous cycle.

So, what is the "X" in "ReLaunch X"

The iterative process of identifying the delta, applying it to the phases of Align, Transform, Monitor, and Measure, followed by identifying the delta again and reapplying it in a continuous iterative manner is the "X" in "ReLaunch X."

"X" is the number of Relaunch Improvement Loops or number of continuous improvement cycles. These completed relaunch loops, or the X in ReLaunch X, would vary from person to person. Higher the X factor means a greater number of Relaunch Improvement Loops completed, and higher will be your probability of successfully completing the transformation journey.

The continuous improvement process is an ongoing cycle that can be applied across various aspects of your life with the single objective of fulfiling your life purpose. The aspects of your life could vary from health to career, family, friends, relationship, financials, and more.

It is important to understand what happens in the Relaunch Improvement Loop (RIL) to appreciate the value of it. The delta you identified feeds back into your Align phase and helps you realign your plans. The realignment could be major, minor, or just a few tweaks. The deltas at first will generally force major changes and alignment. This gets refined over multiple cycles and the delta gets minor. At times, external forces disrupt plans and move it to a major delta. The realignment then recalibrates the transformation activities. These activities are continuously monitored and measured to know the new delta. Application of every delta gives you an opportunity to validate and reinforce your life purpose to make sure it resonates with you.

The RIL is shown as dotted lines in the ReLaunch X framework below.

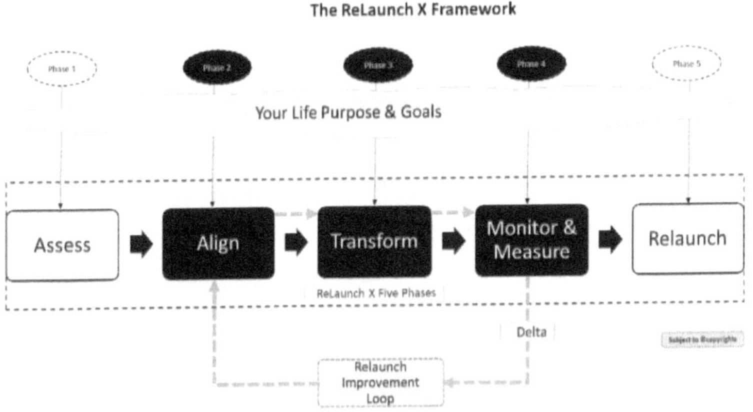

Put differently, the Relaunch Improvement Loop (RIL) is an ongoing process in the transformation journey. At the core of the RIL is the continuous improvement that drives optimisation and over time makes room for new innovation, which in turn drives transformation.

The RIL applies to all goals and should be in full alignment with your life purpose, vision, and mission. The goals could be across professional, financial, personal, family, health, or education sectors, among others. The key is to track the deltas impacting progress towards achievement of your goals, and constructively managing the disruptions by innovatively transforming to relaunch yourself.

At any given point in time, individuals could have multiple relaunch loops addressing different goals or could have a single relaunch loop addressing multiple goals. Once the process is set, the momentum will take the individual to a high degree of awareness, both internally and externally, and will move them into an autopilot mode of the RIL. The loop is an ongoing orbit that perpetually continues.

The RIL not only drives continuous improvements but also helps to anticipate risks and hurdles ahead of time. It works like an early warning system to proactively guide you on what must be done to keep you on track towards achievement of your goals. It drives higher predictability in outcomes along with the consistency of getting work done on time. It eliminates procrastination and increases both efficiency and effectiveness. When used frequently, it will also help to anticipate the impact from external factors, thereby helping to manage both internal and external factors. The relaunch loop works like a smart algorithm. With every cycle, it gets smarter and smoothens your transformation journey.

7.3 The Art of Follow Up

*Diligent follow up and follow through
will set you apart from the crowd and
communicate excellence.*

—John Maxell

Persistence is the trademark of a transformation journey. Successful individuals persist no matter what hurdles lie ahead of them or beside them. They persist until they overcome the hurdles, complete their tasks, and achieve their goals.

To be persistent, you must have a "never say die" attitude. One is reminded of the German football team who always carry a never say die attitude. No matter what the score line, they play their game with perfection as planned.

At the back of persistence is the secret ingredient called *follow up*. Some individuals are inborn with the *follow-up* trait, while others need to acquire it. In either case, individuals must always adopt and carry it with them. One might be tempted to think how in the world is it possible to follow up on all tasks and with everyone. The key is to develop "follow up" as a habit and a way of life. The below steps will help you develop the art of follow up.

1. *Know what to follow up.* At times individuals are lost in their follow up. They get overwhelmed by the pressure to complete their tasks and reach their milestones. They

get distracted by other important tasks that have now become urgent. The net result is that their efforts are ineffective, they lose control, and even worse, they fall behind their plans.

Bottom line: Know what to follow up on, prepare a follow-up list, and ensure it is aligned with your goals.

2. *Prioritise your list*. Having listed down what one needs to follow up on, the next step is to prioritise them. This will ensure you follow up on the high-priority tasks that are critical and have other dependent tasks. You will be far more effective and able to complete a larger number of tasks.

    Bottom line: Do not start your follow up until you have prioritised.

3. *Plan the follow-up process*. Follow up must be done in a planned and orderly manner. You need to make sure you plan the time of the day to follow up on: the list of people you need to follow up with, resources you need for an effective follow up, and importantly how you will follow up on the tasks.

    Bottom line: Put a follow-up plan with a prioritised list.

4. *Make it a ritual*: The more you follow up, the better will be your progress and the more you will achieve. Follow up should be a routine and a habit. Once it is set in motion, it will become a way of life.

    Bottom line: Make it a daily or weekly or fortnightly ritual.

5. *Write it down*. The amazing power of writing actions down is underrated. When you write things down, you are letting your brain know that this is a serious stuff and needs to be retained. Write down what you need to follow up. Once

your follow up is completed, write down the next follow-up actions.

Bottom line: Write down your follow-up activities.

6. *Follow up with yourself.* Set aside a daily time to follow up with yourself. One should develop the habit of first following up with themselves. This would require dedicated time to do a self-review and then follow up with yourself on the tasks assigned to yourself. Imbibing this habit of following up with oneself will influence others around you to do the same.

   Bottom line: Make self follow up a ritual.

7.4 Self-Manage to Relaunch

Many of life's failures are people who did not realise how close they were to success when they gave up.

—Thomas A. Edison

The external factors of disruption have never been higher than before in the history of the world. The rate of newer inventions to address existing needs and simultaneously creating newer needs has been at an all-time high.

The external disruptive factors are forcing organisations and individuals to change the way they work, operate, produce, service, and manage. They have a direct impact on their employees' lives, both at work and at home. On the domestic front, the rapid pace of change in the way children are learning and their fast adoption to new gadgets, apps, and games has further fuelled the inevitable change. The external factors are directly and indirectly driving the internal factors. They are engulfing individuals across the board and forcing them to change, if not transform.

The smart individuals are quick to sense the change ahead of time and proactively plan their actions. Once they have launched their transformation journey, they invest time and effort to self-manage themselves. In its simplest form, self-management is basically leading yourself to achieve your stated goals.

In an organisation, the manager leads his/her team with a common objective of achieving the team's stated goal. This is no different for individuals. There is a great saying that goes, "To lead others you must first lead yourself." Self-management is at the core of our existence.

A student of medicine was once being taught a topic on management. The lecturer was asked a question by the student, "What has management got to do with medicine?" The lecturer responded, "To manage your patients you must first learn to manage yourself." Qualified doctors who have self-managed themselves, along with their emotions and temperament, have been effective in diagnosing, solving problems, treating, and helping their patients recover from different illnesses.

This is no different when managing simple or complex projects. A project manager must self-manage to gain a full control of the situation over the course of the project and his team members. When project milestones are behind schedule, he must be able to think clearly, organise the right resources, take the necessary actions, and bring the project back on track. When project milestones are ahead, he must be able to motivate the teams, proactively identify risks, and mitigate the risks to keep the momentum going. In either case, he must first self-manage and lead himself to be able to lead others.

To self-manage oneself, the key is to understand what needs to be managed and what needs to be leveraged. You need to know your strengths and leverage them to achieve your goals and objectives. You must know your weaknesses to manage the limitations that come along with them. Self-management is about blending the right ingredients to uniquely position you to help achieve your goals. It is about being aware of what is happening within you and around you and then recalibrating yourself to proactively respond.

At the centre of self-management are your core values, which lie below your secondary values. These two value systems, along with managing your strengths and weaknesses, form the fulcrum of self-management. To scale-up self-management to the next level, you must onboard the right qualities that will drive you towards your goals. The qualities acquired over time will become your secondary value system.

The self-management qualities you must onboard include:

1. *Self-awareness.* Be aware of your strengths and limitations, as well as the changes within you and in your ecosystem. Maintain an alert state of mind and be conscious of what to leverage, how to leverage, and who can help you to proactively respond to changes and anticipated disruptions.
2. *Self-esteem.* Believe in your own self and have the confidence to carry on the journey. This is more important when you are sliding down the curve or attempting to recover from a mishap. Ironically at these stages, you tend to have few fans. You need to dig deeper, reflect on your past successes to draw inspiration, and help yourself maintain your self-esteem.
3. *Self-discipline.* Have the discipline to manage self and focus on delivering results. In pursuit of your goals, you can easily lose direction, or get demotivated and derailed. All

because you lacked the discipline to stay the course with an intense focus on delivering the results as per what you had planned.

4. *Empathy.* Value relationships with deep *empathy* for self and others. Developing a strong sense of empathy will invoke your emotional intelligence. Have empathy for yourself and your present situation. Appreciate the fact that you are here because of your thoughts, deeds, and actions. You may be right, wrong, successful, or unsuccessful. You just need to accept, appreciate, and establish empathy for yourself.

   Establishing self-empathy will enable you to develop a deeper sense of understanding others. You will be more empathic to others. Appreciating other people's position touches the human side to reach out and help them. This is fundamental to establishing deep, long-lasting relationships.

   Finding reasons to help and support others will trigger the electric pulse within your network and, in the process, will trigger a stronger pulse in the other person's network. You establish your worthiness in building a stronger network by giving first.

5. *Attitude.* Develop a can-do, will-do approach. Maintaining and managing your energy levels is key to the execution of tasks on time. To achieve this, you must always carry a can-do attitude on one sleeve and a will-do attitude on your other sleeve.

   With your new attitude, you attract success, and it pushes you to carry on with the same momentum. You must value the efforts invested to build the momentum and reach this stage. By the same token, attitude is what carries you out of virtually any situation. This is visibly seen among entrepreneurs. Their can-do and will-do attitude gives them the inner strength and belief to solve any problem coming their way.

6. *Communicate.* Regularly communicate with yourself to be able to communicate with others. To gain clarity of thoughts, take time to reflect daily. Reflect on how you would want your day to unfold and what are the high-priority tasks you must accomplish for the day.

    By midday, take time to reflect on how the day has progressed, what was achieved, and what was missed. By the end of the day, reflect on what were the highs of the day? What tasks could have been done better, and how could you have improved your performance in your discussions and engagements with relevant stakeholders?

    Establishing a ritual of self-reflection will allow you to establish an inner line of communication with yourself. Only when you have clarity of thoughts in your inner communication, will you be able to communicate with the external world. Clarity of thoughts will align your activities and efforts in the direction of achieving your goals and will ensure others around you play a supportive role.

7. Stay committed to acquiring new knowledge for *lifelong learning*. The fast pace of development in this new age digitalised economy and market means that you must move at an even faster pace.

    Only the foolish and ignorant have refused to learn, change, and adapt. The smarter individuals and organisations have been quick to sense the changes around them and are even quicker to respond. They have followed a ritual of daily learning to acquire new knowledge and new skills.

In the process, they have developed new competencies relevant to the current and future marketplace. They have been proactive to generate new ideas and innovate new ways of working and differentiating themselves in the marketplace. They have been at the centre of new innovative initiatives, helping to strategically position both the organisation and themselves.

Smart individuals have made themselves marketable both within their organisations as well as within their industry. They have uniquely placed themselves by committing to continuous lifelong learning.

8. Work with *integrity*. This will earn you lifelong credibility. The only way to build trust is to earn trust. Trust cannot be purchased off-the-shelf. It must be earned step-by-step over the years. Integrity is a core leadership quality. Operating with integrity not only drives the energy within you but it also rubs off on the people around you.

9. *Be agile towards embracing change*. In the earlier days of the information technology (IT) age, the agile methodology enabled IT companies to rapidly develop and deploy software applications, while accommodating new business functionalities into their final product. The success of agile methodology was in its quick win approach. This has now become the cornerstone methodology for start-ups to launch, with their minimal viable products (MVP). The MVP is now widely used in the new age economy by organisations and individuals to drive the pace of innovation. Individuals must take a similar MVP approach of innovating themselves as per their plan, while taking into consideration the new relevant changes that spur around them.

10. Know that *Risks* must be taken and can be managed. Risks are an integral part of rewards. The fundamental rule is without risk there are no rewards. Take banking products for instance; a fixed deposit would fetch you 6–8 per cent return whereas a mutual fund would fetch you 10–17 per cent return, depending on your portfolio.

It is important to comprehend, accept, and onboard the qualities of self-management to continuously relaunch for success.

The value in self-management is to be able to manage the relaunch loop across various facets of an individual's life. With the completion of each iteration, the individual gets better and better. You reach an autopilot state where the mind subconsciously knows what needs to be done at every stage of the transformation journey.

Both individuals and organisations cannot avoid the unpredictability of their transformation journey. They can only prepare themselves for the adventurous ride ahead and continue to successfully relaunch themselves.

Conclusion

The ReLaunch X Framework
Phase 1
Phase 2
Phase 3
Phase 4
Phase 5
Assess
Align
Transform
Monitor & Measure
Relaunch
ReLaunch X Five Phases
Delta
Relaunch Improvement Loop
Subject to copyrights

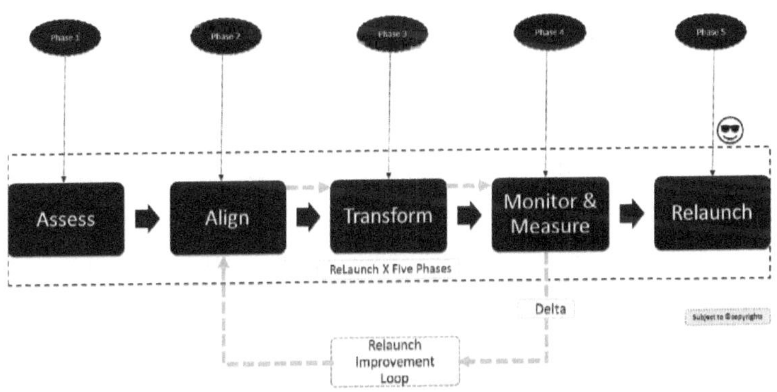

Whatever the mind can conceive and believe,
it can achieve.

—Napoleon Hill

Congratulations! You should be supremely proud of yourself for completing this book. You have achieved what few have accomplished. You dedicated the last few weeks in discovering your life purpose, establishing your goals, transforming, and launching yourself for continued success. You committed to leading yourself through a transformation journey, in fulfilment of your life purpose. In the process, you have now ensured you will reach greater heights in your life and achieve far greater success than you ever imagined.

If you have still not embarked on your transformation journey, remember it is never too late to relaunch yourself. You always have the choice to relaunch yourself at any time in your life. Pick one aspect of your life that needs to be urgently transformed, which, thereby, will help transform the other aspects of your life. It could be professional career, personal finances, health, relationship, family, spouse/partner, or anything else. Just select any one aspect that needs the most attention at this very moment and apply the five phases of ReLaunch X. Nobody is perfect, but if you plan for success, then no matter what, success will follow you, until it is yours. Success begets success!

I urge you to write down the below actions on a sheet of paper and keep it with you for the next ninety days, reading it once daily. This will not only serve you as a reminder but will also get embodied into you. The five takeaway actions are:

1. ***Do not be the rudderless boat.*** Know your life purpose. If you do not have one, you must take the time to ***Assess*** and identify your life purpose. Schedule an appointment with yourself to self-reflect and listen to your inner voice and the untapped passion. This would take a few self-reflection sessions, and you will eventually get there.

2. ***Know your location coordinates.*** Know your "where." ***Align*** where you are now to where you want to be in the future (life purpose) and how you will get there. There is no straight path to your goals and the "points of inflection" will come into play. Be mentally prepared as your transformation journey will have multiple ups, downs, and even temporary moments of pause. It does not matter how slow you move forward, as long as you do not stop or give up. Keep going, and you will make up for the lost momentum when it matters the most.

3. ***You are stronger than you think you are.*** Believe in yourself for others to believe in you. Leverage your strengths and available resources, backed by relentless execution to achieve your goals. The more you progress forward with a can-do and will-do attitude, the more you will ***transform***. Self-management and self-leadership are the super ingredients to turbo-boost your transformation journey. Embrace your transformation journey and cherish the learnings from it. You will successfully complete this journey and be a master of your future transformation journeys.

4. ***Always know your Delta.*** Continuously ***monitor and measure*** your progress against your plans, at regular intervals. Proactively identify and understand how you are progressing in your transformation journey. This will help

you identify what more needs to be done to reach your end goals. Work hard, work smart, and work fast to stay ahead of the game.

5. ***Make relaunch your way of life***. Knowing where you are now and where you want to be, realign your resources and ***Relaunch*** yourself to complete your transformation journey. Remember the Relaunch Improvement Loop (RIL) is an iterative process of identifying the delta, followed by realigning your plans, transforming yourself, and once again monitoring and measuring your progress. Focus on what you can proactively improve every day, even in a small way, to complete your transformation journey.

By mastering the five ReLaunch X phases of Assess, Align, Transformation, Monitor & Measure, and Relaunch, you are now in control of your transformation journey and will live your life in fulfilment of your life purpose.

We cannot control the outcome of the disruptions happening around us, but we can control our minds and how we prepare and respond to them. This disruption has forever changed the way we live, engage, learn, earn, and value our loved ones. It has ensured we unlearn the habits we acquired over the last decade, only to embrace the new values of life for the next decade.

The effect of this pandemic exposed the vulnerability of countries, industries, organisations, and people. Ironically, it also demonstrated how other countries, organisations, and people reacted differently, only to relaunch themselves with sheer determination and persistence. Interestingly, human forces joined hands with the disruptive forces of digitalisation to combat this pandemic disruption. In the process, we have witnessed an unprecedented adoption in digitalisation across all aspects of life. Work from home, online education, and social distancing, among others, have become a new norm, fuelling other disruptive changes. These disruptive changes are forcing companies and industries to not only change their business and operating models but also reskill their existing workforce, thereby redefining the future of work. By embracing disruptions in our lives, we become better equipped to relaunch ourselves not once but several times!

You now have the knowledge of ReLaunch X, the tools, and the power to transform yourself. You owe it to yourself to complete your transformation journey and create your legacy for life. While you transform and earn the benefits of ReLaunch X, make sure you engage with two other people in your life. Teach them the five phases of ReLaunch X and guide them through each phase. The immense satisfaction you will derive will leave you fulfilled in more than many ways. The law of Karma will pay you back, more than you ever imagined!

I would love to hear back from you on how ReLaunch X has helped you in your life and the progress you made in your transformation journey. Mail me your story with the sub: My ReLaunch X Transformation in Motion. You can reach me at *Stephen@Stephenfernandes.com*

Bibliography

The Credit Suisse Research Institute. "Global Wealth Report 2019." Credit Suisse, October 21, 2019. https://www.credit-suisse.com/about-us-news/en/articles/media-releases/global-wealth-report-2019--global-wealth-rises-by-2-6--driven-by-201910.html

Earley, Brigitt. "Here's How Make a Vision Board." Oprahmag Magazine, November 26, 2019. https://www.oprahmag.com/life/a29959841/how-to-make-a-vision-board/.

The Editors of Encyclopaedia Britannica. "Newton's Laws of Motion." Encyclopædia Britannica, February 3, 2020. https://www.britannica.com/science/Newtons-laws-of-motion.

"Enduring Ideas: The GE–McKinsey Nine-Box Matrix." McKinsey Quarterly, September 1, 2008. https://www.mckinsey.com/business-functions/strategy-and-corporate-finance/our-insights/enduring-ideas-the-ge-and-mckinsey-nine-box-matrix#.

"Four Stages of Competence." Wikipedia. https://en.wikipedia.org/wiki/Four_stages_of_competence.

Goleman, Daniel. "Emotional Intelligence." https://www.danielgoleman.info/.

Grant, Mitchell. "Strength, Weakness, Opportunity, and Threat (SWOT) Analysis." Reviewed by Gordon Scott. Investopedia, February 24, 2020. https://www.investopedia.com/terms/s/swot.asp.

How To Use A Vision Board To Grow Your Business, September 14 2012. Beverly Jones. http://www.microbusinesshub.co.uk/vision-boards/

Hill, Napoleon. *The Law of Success*. Tribeca Books, 1928. https://en.wikipedia.org/wiki/The_Law_of_Success.

Investopedia Staff. 2019. "Pareto Principle." Investopedia, August 29, 2019. https://www.investopedia.com/terms/p/paretoprinciple.asp.

Jones, Beverly. "How to Use a Vision Board to Grow Your Business." Micro Business Hub, September 14, 2012. http://www.microbusinesshub.co.uk/vision-boards/.

Kaplan, Robert S., and Norton, David P. "The Balanced Scorecard—Measures that Drive Performance." *Harvard Business Review*, January–February 1992. https://hbr.org/1992/01/the-balanced-scorecard-measures-that-drive-performance-2.

Kübler-Ross, Elisabeth. "Kübler-Ross Change Curve®." Elisabeth Kübler-Ross Foundation. https://www.ekrfoundation.org/5-stages-of-grief/change-curve/.

Lea, Seán. "GROW Model." Businessballs, November 1, 2018. https://www.businessballs.com/coaching-and-mentoring/grow-model/.

Lynch, John. "A 7-Year-Old Boy Is Making $11 Million a Year on YouTube Reviewing Toys." *Business Insider*, July 19, 2018. https://www.businessinsider.com/ryan-toysreview-6-year-old-makes-11-million-per-year-youtube-2017-12.

Mind Tools Content Team. "PEST Analysis: Identifying 'Big Picture' Opportunities and Threats." MindTools. https://www.mindtools.com/pages/article/newTMC_09.htm.

Mind Tools Content Team. "SMART Goals: How to Make Your Goals Achievable." MindTools. https://www.mindtools.com/pages/article/smart-goals.htm.

The Roller-Coaster Ride. Image Source: https://www.baltimoremagazine.com/2014/8/11/amusement-park-ride-roundup

Product Lifecycle. https://www.quora.com/What-is-the-product-life-cycle

Schwartz, Tony, and Catherine McCarthy. "Manage Your Energy, Not Your Time." *Harvard Business Review*, October 2007. https://hbr.org/2007/10/manage-your-energy-not-your-time.

Wroblewski, M. T. "A Theory of Goal Setting By Locke & Latham." Chron, January 28, 2019. https://smallbusiness.chron.com/theory-goal-setting-locke-latham-1879.html.

www.ingramcontent.com/pod-product-compliance
Lightning Source LLC
Chambersburg PA
CBHW032223050726
47591CB00001B/231